895

P9-BJW-641

THE GREAT SIGHTS OF
NEW YORK
A Photographic Guide

THE GREAT SIGHTS OF NEW YORK

A Photographic Guide

Second, Revised Edition

Text by
JAMES SPERO

Photographs by
EDMUND V. GILLON, Jr.

Foreword by Mayor Edward I. Koch

Dover Publications, Inc.
New York

For my mother and father
SHIRLEY AND EUGENE SPERO
Even though they prefer the Little Mango to the Big Apple

Frontispiece. The island of Manhattan, looking south across Madison Square. To the left of the twin towers of the World Trade Center, in the Upper Bay is the Verrazano-Narrows Bridge. To the right of the towers is the Statue of Liberty.

Copyright © 1979, 1991 by Dover Publications, Inc.
All rights reserved under Pan American and International Copyright Conventions.

Published in Canada by General Publishing Company, Ltd., 30 Lesmill Road, Don Mills, Toronto, Ontario.
Published in the United Kingdom by Constable and Company, Ltd., 3 The Lanchesters, 162–164 Fulham Palace Road, London W6 9ER.

This Dover edition, first published in 1991, is a revised edition of the work originally published by Dover Publications, Inc., in 1979.

Book design by Carol Belanger Grafton

Manufactured in the United States of America
Dover Publications, Inc., 31 East 2nd Street, Mineola, N.Y. 11501

Library of Congress Cataloging-in-Publication Data

Spero, James.
    The great sights of New York : a photographic guide / text by James Spero, photographs by Edmund V. Gillon. Jr. : Foreword by Edward I. Koch. — 2nd. rev. ed.
        p.   cm.
    Includes index.
    ISBN 0-486-26727-X (pbk.)
    1. New York (N.Y.)—Description—1981– —Views.
    I. Gillon, Edmund Vincent.   II. Title.
    F128.37.S68   1991
    917.47'10443—dc20
                                                    91-13284
                                                    CIP

INTRODUCTION

New York is a vortex, a city of relentless change. This is its excitement, its endless allure and, paradoxically, its main tradition. The city as it was known to our great-grandparents 75 years ago has changed almost beyond recognition; an astonishing number of the landmarks by which they related to it are gone. Massive Pennsylvania Station, built by McKim, Mead and White to last a thousand years, did not endure even a century. But as fast as buildings come crashing down, new ones rise. If the old Metropolitan Opera House fell to the wrecker's ball, Lincoln Center has become a moving force in the performing arts; if the skyline of lower Manhattan lost the Singer Building, it has gained the unmistakable profile of the World Trade Center.

This book presents 102 of the most outstanding sights in New York today, relates basic information about them and shows how they figure in the history and fabric of the city. That there are more than 102 sights in the city worthy of notice should be obvious; selecting the ones included here was a difficult task. The attempt was made to present aspects of the city that would appeal to different interests—historical, social, financial and business, artistic and architectural. While most readers should find all they expect here, it is inevitable that some will find a few of their personal favorites missing. I can only offer them my apologies and the assurance that some of mine were sacrificed to attain a balance.

I have tried to keep my text as objective and factual as possible, but it is unavoidable that some personal bias may have crept into it. Any value judgments are mine alone, and are not those of the publisher. Nor is the mention of any commercial establishment intended to imply an endorsement by myself or by Dover Publications.

I owe thanks to New Yorkers, too numerous to mention individually, who were generous with their time and information. It was Ned Melman who conceived of the book; Ed Gillon helped me see the city through fresh eyes; Hayward Cirker, a consummate New Yorker, offered encouragement and advice; and Mayor Koch took time from his frantic schedule to write the Foreword.

J.S.

INTRODUCTION TO THE SECOND EDITION

Since the publication of this book in 1979, New York City has gone full circle on Fortune's wheel. Just emerging from a financial crisis, it was about to experience a decade of boom before hitting the skids again. Ten years of frenetic real-estate development left great changes in the face of the city: What had been, until recently, a part of the Hudson River seemed to pop up as Battery Park City—almost too sleek and pristine to be part of New York. And seemingly imperishable institutions, such as Altman's and Gimbel's, became memories. In this second edition I have tried to keep track of the changes the intervening years—fat and lean—have wrought upon the city.

J.S.

FOREWORD
By Mayor Edward I. Koch

From its earliest days, New York has been a city of great sights. The natural splendor of our environment, our 575 miles of waterfront, and our economically vital location on one of the world's great harbors have all joined together to produce an exciting city which has in turn inspired the genius of those who live and work here.

There are thousands of great sights in New York, and some of the most outstanding ones have been included in this volume. If you like the pictures, however, you will love seeing the sights in person. Over 17 million people visit New York every year, and this book will give you a good idea why.

ALPHABETICAL LIST OF SIGHTS

(References are to item numbers)

CONTENTS

The following contents is a list of the great sights of New York in the order in which they appear in this book. The numbers are also used to identify the sights on the map of Manhattan on the following two pages. Numbers outside Manhattan are not included on the map.

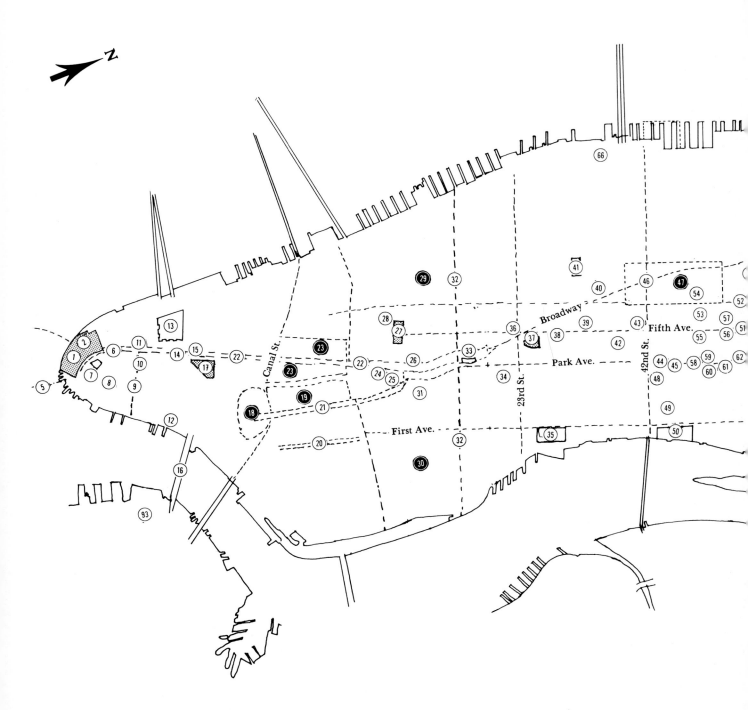

MAP OF MANHATTAN

Numbers refer to items listed on the preceding page.

For adjoining area see inset.

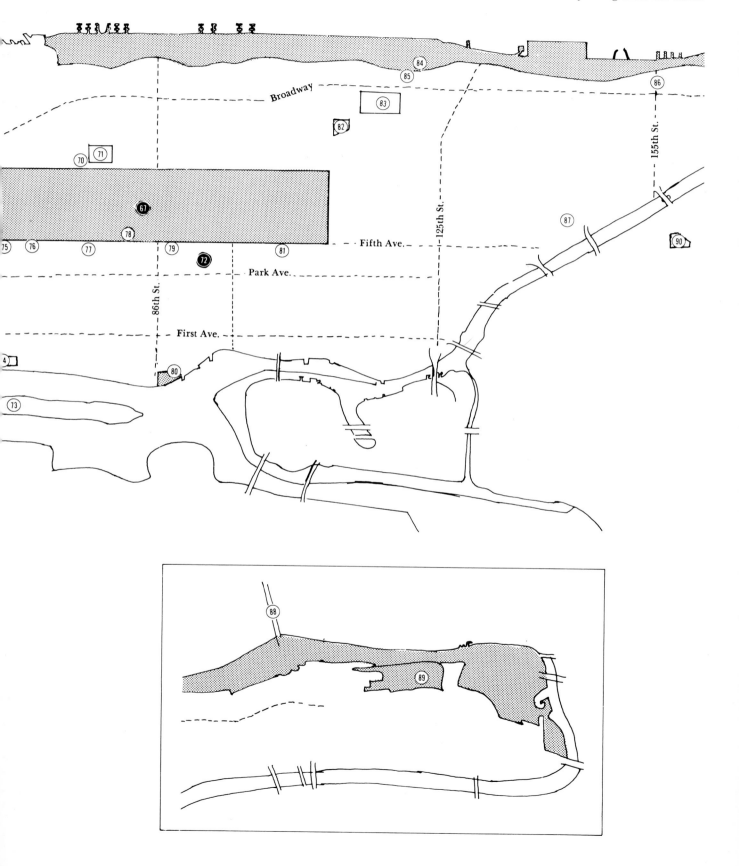

THE GREAT SIGHTS OF
NEW YORK
A Photographic Guide

1. Battery Park. At the southern tip of Manhattan, Battery Park is one of New York's most delightful public spaces. The park takes its name from the battery of cannon that stood along the shore in 1683–85. At that time the shoreline ran where State Street is today. The park has undergone considerable growth through landfill and many alterations. Early in the nineteenth century it was an extremely fashionable promenade. It also attracted crowds of amusement seekers as the location of Castle Garden, which stood not far offshore (subsequent landfill has left it high and dry; see No. 2). The popularity of the park has not abated. Tourists visiting New York are sure to see it on their way to the Statue of Liberty or Ellis Island (boats for which leave from the park; see Nos. 3 & 4). New Yorkers never cease to take delight in its sweeping views of the harbor and the refreshing breezes that usually blow there, even in the hottest weather. Each day thousands of Staten Islanders see it as they commute to and from Manhattan on the ferry. The park is dotted with many statues and memo-

rials connected with New York's history and maritime traditions. Jonathan Scott Hartley's statue of John Ericsson (1893) shows the engineer holding a model of the famous ironclad ship *Monitor*, which he designed and had built in the Brooklyn Navy Yard, across the East River. The bust of Giovanni da Verrazano by Ettore Ximenes (1909) is a tribute to the first European to sight New York's waters (1524). A monument donated by the Dutch government commemorates the settlement of New Amsterdam (1625), most of which was centered around nearby Bowling Green. The John W. Ambrose Memorial honors the man who engineered the dredging of the channel which afforded large ships easy access to the harbor. The largest memorial is the East Coast War Memorial, designed by William Gehron and dedicated in 1960. Dominated by a huge eagle, it lists the names of the members of the armed forces who died in American coastal waters of the North Atlantic during the Second World War.

2. Castle Clinton National Monument, Battery Park. Originally named West Battery, the fort was built in 1807, when deteriorating relations with England made New York apprehensive for its safety. Designed by John McComb, Jr. (also one of the architects of City Hall), the fort was built 200 yards offshore and was connected to the mainland by a causeway. It was not made part of the park, by landfill, until the middle of the century. The fort, along with Castle Williams, which stands opposite on Governors Island, was never called upon to defend the city in the War of 1812. In 1815 it was renamed to honor DeWitt Clinton, who later, as Governor of New York, was the guiding spirit behind the Erie Canal. The City leased the fort from the federal government in 1824, redecorated it with shrubs and a fountain and opened it to the public as Castle Garden, which became a popular amusement spot. The building underwent another transformation in 1845, when it was roofed over and made into a concert hall. P. T. Barnum scored a triumph when he had Jenny Lind sing her first American concert there on September 11, 1850; the great impresario's publicity for the event had been handled so skillfully that New York was whipped into a frenzy over the "Swedish Nightingale." From 1855 until 1890 the former fort served as the immigration center for New York; it was closed when Ellis Island (No. 3) took over the function. In 1896, after remodeling, the building opened as the New York Aquarium, which it remained until the early 1940s. The Aquarium has moved to newer, more spacious quarters in Coney Island (No. 98). To save Castle Clinton from threatened destruction, Congress designated it a national historic monument in 1946, but it remained closed. Finally, in 1976, it was reopened to the public, restored to its original condition.

3. Ellis Island, Upper New York Bay. Between 1855 and 1890 Castle Clinton, on the Battery, served as New York's immigration station. In its years of operation it processed over eight million arrivals, but it proved unequal to the great waves of immigrants who poured into the station as the century advanced toward its close. In 1892 the federal government, having assumed control of immigration from the city, opened a new facility on six-acre Ellis Island. The fancifully turreted Immigration Station, seen here, was designed by Boring & Tilton and opened in 1898. To newly arrived immigrants it represented the last, and perhaps most frightening, barrier to cross before they could enter the New World. For it was here that immigration officials carried out their duties to "see that the provisions of the laws forbidding the landing of certain prohibited classes, namely: convicts, lunatics, idiots, paupers, persons likely to become public charges, or suffering with contagious or loathsome diseases, contract laborers, and polygamists, are carried out" (*King's Handbook of New York City*, 1893). In 1907, the peak year of immigration, 1,285,349 immigrants were admitted. With increasing restrictions on immigration, the number declined, and in 1954, after processing between 12 and 16 million immigrants, the station was closed and left to decay. The island was subsequently designated a National Shrine. In 1990, after extensive restoration, part of the island, including the Immigration Station, was opened to the public on a year-round basis. It is well worth seeing, especially for those whose forebears passed through it on their way to establishing new lives in this country.

4. Statue of Liberty, Liberty Island, Upper New York Bay *(opposite).* In 1865 the noted sculptor Frédéric-Auguste Bartholdi discussed with a group of his friends in Paris the possibility of a gift to America from France to commemorate the friendship of the two nations and to celebrate the freedom revered by both peoples. The idea of a colossal statue was eventually conceived. A committee was organized and the French people donated the $200,000 Bartholdi needed to execute this monumental task. He first modeled the work in terra-cotta (probably using his mother as a model) and then made four successive enlargements. The final statue, assembled from repoussé copper, eventually rose over the rooftops of Paris. The official ceremony of presentation to the American people was held on July 4, 1884. The French frigate *Isère* carried the 350 dismantled pieces to the United States, but years passed before the statue was erected. The French had been quick to finance the creation of the statue; the Americans were considerably slower in contributing the $250,000 needed to have it erected. Through the efforts of many individuals (notably Joseph Pulitzer, who gave the cause much publicity in his newspaper, *The World*) the money was finally raised. The statue was erected on Bedloe's Island, on which pirates had once been hanged, and which later served as a fortification protecting the Hudson. The pedestal, by noted architect Richard Morris Hunt, was built atop star-shaped Fort Wood, which dates from 1841. The statue's framework was engineered by Gustave Eiffel, who later designed the famous tower in Paris which bears his name. On October 28, 1886, President Grover Cleveland dedicated the statue, which is officially titled *Liberty Enlightening the World.* Since then millions have made the pilgrimage to visit her. A few figures give an idea of the enormous proportions of the statue and its base. The height from base to torch is 151 feet. The height from the foundation of the pedestal to the torch is 305 feet. From heel to top of head the figure towers 111 feet. The length of her index finger is 8 feet. Her mouth is 3 feet wide. Her right arm is 42 feet long. She weighs 225 tons (100 tons of copper and 125 tons of structural steel). Visitors may climb into her head for a spectacular view of New York Harbor, but the torch has been closed to the public since 1916. At night the statue is floodlighted. On the base of the statue is affixed a plaque bearing Emma Lazarus' famous poem "The New Colossus," written in 1883; it contains the famous lines: "Give me your tired, your poor,/Your huddled masses yearning to breathe free. . . ." The statue is one of the most powerful symbols ever created. As millions of immigrants entered the country at the turn of the century, it was the first important structure they saw, the first emotional and esthetic experience of their adventure in a new land.

5. Staten Island Ferry (from the Battery to St. George) *(above).*

> We were very tired, we were very merry,
> We had gone back and forth all night on the ferry.

New Yorkers still delight in the ferry, as did Edna St. Vincent Millay when she wrote these lines years ago. The only mass-transportation link between Staten Island and Manhattan, this is the last major ferry line in a city whose rivers once bristled with ferries. It dates back to the year 1810, when 16-year-old Cornelius Vanderbilt borrowed $100 from his mother to launch the business. By the end of the first year he had cleared a profit of $1,000, and his amazing career was under way. The ferry remained in private hands until 1905. It was then purchased by the city, which continued the now-legendary fare of a nickel, established in 1897. The fare finally fell victim to inflation in 1975, when a round-trip fare of 25 cents was instituted. (That fare, in turn, has become but a memory.) The fleet has had an enviable performance record; 95 percent of its trips are completed on time, and ferries even ran during the hurricanes of 1938 and 1972. In half a century, during which the line has carried about one billion passengers five billion passenger miles, there have been no fatal accidents. In addition to its 3,500 seated passengers, each ferry accommodates between 25 and 45 cars. During rush hour, about 18,000 passengers are brought into Manhattan. The trip, which starts in Manhattan at the terminal near the Battery, lasts 25 minutes and offers views of Governors Island, the Statue of Liberty and Ellis Island, as well as the spectacular panorama of lower Manhattan seen here.

6. Bowling Green, Foot of Broadway. The juxtaposition of the tiny, charming park and the looming buildings of the financial district dramatically demonstrates New York's meteoric growth. The site was first used in 1638 as part of the Dutch colony's cattle market. It was later a parade ground. In 1733 the city Common Council leased it at an annual rent of one peppercorn to three men who developed it as a bowling green for public amusement. It thus became New York's first public park. The area became fashionable, and at various times such luminaries as Lords Howe and Cornwallis, Benedict Arnold, Talleyrand and Washington resided in houses on or near the Green. In 1771 the park was enclosed by a fence to protect the newly erected equestrian statue of George III. The statue stood until July 9, 1776, when the Declaration of Independence was read to inflamed New Yorkers, who pulled it down for use in making bullets (fragments of the statue are on display in the New-York Historical Society, No. 70). The fence had better luck; the royal crowns that topped some of its posts were knocked down, but otherwise it has survived to the present. The park underwent many changes in the following years, but was fully restored to include a fountain and was reopened to the public in 1977. Today it fulfills the same purpose it did in 1733—as a place for New Yorkers to recreate themselves—and this small piece of virgin soil has remained essentially unchanged for hundreds of years.

7. Former United States Custom House, Bowling Green.
Monumentality, a profusion of dramatic sculpture and richly textured and ornamented surfaces combine to make the Custom House one of the finest Beaux-Arts buildings in New York. Its site, bounded by Bowling Green and State, Bridge and Whitehall Streets, is rich in New York history. It was there that the first rudimentary Dutch defenses were built in 1626, to be replaced by Fort Amsterdam in 1635. This fort, which enclosed the principal buildings of the tiny colony of New Amsterdam, was large enough so that the entire population could take refuge within it in times of danger. In 1787 a mansion, designed as a residence for the President, was erected on the site; but when the capital was moved to Philadelphia, the structure became the residence of the Governor of New York. In 1799 it became the United States Custom House but in 1814 it was demolished by fire and the offices were moved. In 1892 the historic spot was purchased by the U.S. Treasury as a site for an important new Custom House in keeping with the position the nation had assumed in world trade. A competition held for its design was won by Cass Gilbert, who later designed the Woolworth Building (see

No. 15). The Custom House was completed in 1907. The main facade, fronting Bowling Green, features four excellent sculptures, *The Four Continents*, by Daniel Chester French. The allegorical groupings depict Africa, Asia, Europe and America (seen in the photograph). The 12 heroic-sized statues on the cornice represent nations that have prospered in maritime trade. The building's interior is correspondingly opulent. The impressive rotunda is one of the city's finest rooms; its murals, depicting the progress of a ship entering the harbor, were executed by Reginald Marsh in 1937. The building has stood vacant since the U.S. Customs Service moved to the World Trade Center (No. 13). The interior of the old building was opened to the public in 1976 and during the summers of 1977 and 1979. In the late 1980s, when it was decided that the Museum of the American Indian would transfer the bulk of its collection from its premises in Audubon Terrace to Washington, D.C., the old Custom House was designated as the place in Manhattan where some of the collection would be on display. Most of the building, however, is used for offices.

8. Fraunces Tavern, Broad and Pearl Streets *(above).* The romance of America's Revolutionary past hovers around Fraunces Tavern at No. 54 Broad Street. In 1719 the building was erected as the home of Huguenot nobleman Etienne de Lancey, who lived in it until 1730. In 1762 a West Indian Creole named "Black Sam" Fraunces, who later became George Washington's steward, bought the house and ran it as one of his roadhouses, calling it the Queen's Head Tavern. In this building Washington bade farewell to his officers on December 4, 1783. Fraunces sold the tavern two years later. In the nineteenth century the structure underwent extensive alterations and managed to survive two fires. By the time the Sons of the Revolution purchased it, only parts of the walls and an indication of the roof line remained to aid William Mersereau in his 1907 "restoration" of the tavern, which was actually guesswork with regard to the original appearance. As pleasant as the building is, it should be valued more for its associations than as an authentic artifact of the eighteenth century. A popular restaurant operates on the premises; a small museum with Revolutionary memorabilia, including a lock of Washington's hair, is located on the third floor. Behind the tavern rises the First National City Trust Co. at No. 20 Exchange Place (1931; Cross & Cross, architects), an interesting example of a skyscraper in the Art Deco style.

9. Wall Street *(opposite).* In 1653, alarmed by the possibility that the war being waged between Holland and England might affect New Amsterdam, Governor Peter Stuyvesant strengthened the fortifications of the little colony. His precautions included the construction of a wall to the north of the city. The wall was never used as a defense, either against the Indians or against the English, who took the city in 1664 without bloodshed or battle. The old wall deteriorated and was eventually pulled down, but the name stuck and today Wall Street, as the center of one of the world's greatest financial districts, has become synonymous with the capitalist system. The street first became an important part of the city in 1699, when work began on a new City Hall at Wall and Nassau Streets. In 1709 a market was established, giving the street a commercial note. The Tontine Coffee House was built there in 1792–94. Under a buttonwood tree that grew near the coffee house, 24 brokers drew up a trading agreement establishing what developed into the New York Stock Exchange. The Exchange, the world's largest, now occupies the building at the left edge of the picture, No. 8 Broad Street. Designed in 1903 by George B. Post, it was enlarged in 1923. In the course of the tours that are offered, some of the complexities of the system are explained. In addition, the Visitor's Gallery gives the tourist a chance to observe the organized chaos on the floor of the Exchange. The market is now closely regulated, so there is little chance of a recurrence of the panics that turned Wall Street into a seething mass of frantic brokers several times in the past. This view, looking up Wall Street from the Federal Hall National Memorial (No. 10), shows Trinity Church (No. 11) at Broadway, seemingly sandwiched between the buildings that form the famous "canyons" of lower Manhattan. Through the middle of the nineteenth century the church's spire was the tallest structure on the island and a reference point by which most travel directions were given.

10. Federal Hall National Memorial, Wall and Nassau Streets
(above). The Federal Hall National Memorial stands on one
of the nation's most historic sites. It was there that New
York's City Hall was built in 1699–1701. Within that structure Andrew Hamilton argued Peter Zenger's famous free-
dom-of-the-press case in 1735. "Taxation without rep-
resentation" was bitterly assailed there by the Stamp Act
Congress in 1765. In 1787 work on the Constitution of the
new nation was finished there. In 1788 the building was completely remodeled as Federal Hall, the first Capitol of the
United States, by Pierre L'Enfant, who later laid out the plan
of Washington, D.C. On its balcony George Washington was
inaugurated as first President on April 30, 1789. The eigh-
teenth-century building was eventually razed; in 1833–42
the present structure was erected on the site as the U.S.
Custom House. The exterior, designed by Town and Davis, is
probably the finest example of the Greek Revival style in New
York. Reflecting the massive severity of the Doric order, it
was built of marble quarried in Massachusetts. The outstanding interior (the architect is not identified with certain-
ty) features a rotunda and skylight. The statue by John Q. A.
Ward on the building's steps, unveiled by Governor Grover
Cleveland in 1883 in the presence of President Chester A. Arthur, portrays Washington taking the oath of office, and is
located in the approximate spot where the event took place. A
block of masonry from old Federal Hall, on which Washington is supposed to have stood during the ceremony, is incorporated in the pedestal.

11. Trinity Church, Broadway and Wall Street *(opposite).* The
brownstone Gothic Revival church is the third to stand on the
spot. The first was completed in 1697. The notorious Captain

Kidd was among those who made obligatory contributions
toward its construction. The land grant for Trinity Parish did
not come from Queen Anne until 1705. Because of the extent
of the grant and years of skillful investment, Trinity is probably the city's wealthiest parish. The first church was
destroyed in the fire of 1776, which ravaged much of the city
when the Revolutionaries left New York and the British took
occupation. The second building had to be demolished because of structural deficiencies. The present church, completed in 1846, was designed by Richard Upjohn, who was
greatly influenced by the work of Augustus W. Pugin, the
English architect most famous for his work on the Houses of
Parliament. The building has received later artistic embel-
lishments. The bronze doors, designed by Richard Morris
Hunt, were inspired by Ghiberti's "Doors of Paradise" on the
Baptistery in Florence. The sculpture on the doors is the work
of three distinguished artists, John Massey Rhind (right), Karl
Bitter (center) and Charles Niehaus (left); Bitter included a
portrait of Hunt in his work. The churchyard covers 2½
acres; the oldest surviving tombstone, that of Richard
Churcher, was erected in 1681, antedating the first church
building. Among the famous who lie buried in the churchyard are Alexander Hamilton, Robert Fulton and Captain
James Lawrence. The Martyrs' Monument (1852) commemorates the American soldiers, now interred in the
churchyard, who died while imprisoned by the British in the
old Rhinelander sugar warehouse that stood on Liberty
Street. At lunchtime during the week the churchyard is a
refuge for office workers, a permanent historic oasis in a
desert of brick and cement.

12. South Street Seaport Museum, East River around Fulton Street *(above).* The age of sail lives again in New York at the South Street Seaport Museum, an enclave of seven blocks along the East River that embraces piers, ships, aged storehouses and the Fulton Market. It has received landmark designation; the boundaries are the river to the east, Peck Slip to the north, Water Street to the west and John Street to the south. The area was the heart of the young nation's maritime trade in the first half of the nineteenth century. The elegant Greek Revival countinghouses, a few of which survive, held the offices of the merchants whose trade widened until it included China and Japan. It was these merchants who played a major role in establishing New York's position as the leading city of the United States. After the Civil War, international shipping moved to the Hudson River, and South Street went into a decline. With the building boom of the 1960s the old buildings that filled the area were fast disappearing, and it is fortunate that the area was set aside and the museum established to preserve what it could of this unique aspect of New York's history. The South Street Seaport Museum has quickly become one of the city's most active and popular cultural centers. Not only does it hold permanent and temporary exhibitions focusing on the city and its maritime trade, but it also sponsors events such as folk dances and plays. In this photograph the bowsprit of the museum's metal-hulled *Wavertree,* built in England in 1885, soars over Pier 16, where the museum has gathered a variety of ships, including a tugboat, the schooner *Pioneer* and the lightship *Ambrose.* In the distance is the square-rigger *Peking.* The expansion of commercial space has also made the area a favorite for shopping.

13. World Trade Center, West Street North of Liberty Street *(opposite).* The World Trade Center, along with Battery Park City, comprises the most spectacular building project to have been executed in New York in recent times. Dominated by the 1,350-foot twin towers, the World Trade Center was financed and is run by the Port Authority as a focal point for international trade in the hope that the center will not only maintain but increase the importance of the harbor in trade. The project was approved by the state legislatures of New York and New Jersey in 1962. Construction of the two towers involved the excavation of more than 1.2 million cubic yards of earth and rock. This material was added to the 95-acre landfill along the Hudson to build Battery Park City, which consists of the World Financial Center and residential areas (this view having been taken from the South Residential Quadrant), built in styles echoing those of the past. A delightful esplanade runs along the river, offering strollers a walk in cool river breezes during hot weather. New construction techniques had to be developed to erect the twin towers, designed by Minoru Yamasaki and Emery Roth and Sons. The exterior wall of each building is load-bearing (in conventional skyscrapers, the load is borne by a steel skeleton). A computer constantly monitors lighting and temperature conditions within the buildings. Shops and restaurants in the concourse provide services to the center's 50,000 employees—more than the total population of Manhattan at the time of the Revolution. Atop the complex, a luxury restaurant, Windows on the World, offers spectacular views with its meals. Visitors simply interested in the view can go to the observation deck above the 100th floor of Number Two to enjoy the views of Manhattan, New Jersey, Brooklyn and the harbor. The twin towers have offered an irresistible temptation to adventurers. One has walked across a wire strung between the tops of the two buildings. Another, a "human fly," scaled the edge of the South Tower, making it to the top.

14. St. Paul's Chapel, Broadway between Fulton and Vesey Streets *(opposite)*. This is the only building that survives from New York City as it existed before the Revolution. All the others fell victim to disastrous fires or New York's relentless growth. The handsome Georgian building, completed in 1766, was designed by Thomas McBean, a pupil of James Gibbs. It is obvious that McBean took as his model his teacher's design for St. Martin-in-the-Fields in Trafalgar Square, London. The Broadway entrance was designed as a secondary one. The principal entrance was placed at the opposite end because of the magnificent view of the Hudson it commanded at the time. The steeple, designed by James Crommelin Lawrence, was erected in 1796. The elegant interior was, for the most part, the work of Pierre L'Enfant, who also redesigned Federal Hall (No. 10). The beautiful pillars, chandeliers of Waterford cut glass, pulpit, and altar with a "glory" above it are all outstanding. The device above the altar with the three plumes of the Prince of Wales is all that remains in the city to remind it of its former royal masters. The chapel has counted many famous people among its worshippers, foremost being George Washington (his pew is on the north aisle). Others were William IV (when Prince of Wales), Major John André, Lord Cornwallis, Lord Howe, the Marquis de Lafayette and Presidents Cleveland and Harrison.

15. Woolworth Building, Broadway between Barclay Street and Park Place *(above)*. Seen from beneath the arches of the Municipal Building and backed by the World Trade Center, the 729-foot-tall Woolworth Building rises into the downtown skyline. Located at No. 233 Broadway, the 60-story building was the tallest in the world from its opening in 1913 until 1930, when the Chrysler Building claimed the title. The structure carried out the dream of Frank Woolworth (1852–1919), founder of the chain of five-and-ten-cent stores, who paid the 15.5-million-dollar construction fee in cash. Dealing with the problem of designing so tall a building in a prestigious Beaux-Arts style, architect Cass Gilbert stressed its verticality with a terra-cotta Gothic facade rich in ornamentation, including humorous gargoyles caricaturing himself and Woolworth, among others. It was only natural that the building should be described as a "cathedral of commerce." The lobby is one of the most beautiful in the city. The cupola of City Hall can be seen rising over the top of the trees at the bottom of the photograph.

16. Brooklyn Bridge. Universally acknowledged as one of the great engineering triumphs of all time, Brooklyn Bridge links Manhattan's City Hall Park to Cadman Plaza in Brooklyn; the view here is from the Brooklyn side. Until the bridge was built, many ferries, notably the Fulton Ferry, carried the heavy traffic between the city of Brooklyn and the city of New York (it was not until 1898, with the creation of Greater New York, that Brooklyn became a mere borough). The bridge is a memorial to its two creators, John A. Roebling, a German immigrant, and his son Washington. John conceived of the bridge and saw it through its planning stages but was killed in an accident when he was taking sightings for the project in 1869. His son Washington carried the project to completion. Actual construction began in 1870. The undertaking was tremendous, considering the scope of the project, the technology of the time and the lack of precedent for so large a suspension bridge. The sandhogs who labored in the depths on the foundations for the piers were frequently victims of caisson disease, the bends, for which there was then no effective treatment. Washington Roebling was himself a victim. His health shattered by the disease and the grueling workload he maintained, he had to supervise much of the construction from his home a few blocks from the site on the Brooklyn side, using a telescope and sending his instructions by messenger. The bridge's opening in 1883 was celebrated with ceremonies attended by President Arthur and with a magnificent display of fireworks. The bridge's maximum length of span is 1,595.5 feet; its maximum clearance above mean high water is 133 feet. The piers, designed in the Gothic Revival style, are built of pinkish granite. The bridge cost over $16 million to construct, which was an enormous amount at the time, some of the money going into the pocket of the notorious Boss Tweed. Since its opening 45 people have jumped from the bridge; only 11 have survived (Steve Brodie's claim may be spurious). The trollies that once crossed the bridge have ceased operation, but its pedestrian walk remains, offering spectacular views of the Manhattan skyline.

17. City Hall, City Hall Park. An outstanding piece of architecture, the New York City Hall was the collaboration of a Frenchman, Joseph Mangin, and a Scot, John McComb, Jr. Consequently, although the building is generally Federal in style, it shows a strong French influence. When City Hall was built in 1812, the population of New York City was a bit over 120,000 and the inhabited area north of Canal Street was chiefly farmland. The municipal government has since grown so large that the building can only accommodate a small fraction of it. City Hall had become so dilapidated that in 1959 a complete renovation was carried out by the firm of Shreve, Lamb & Harmon. The eroded marble of the south facade was replaced with Alabama limestone, as was the north facade. That facade was originally built in brownstone; the building stood so far north at the time, the city fathers felt that few people would go around to the back of the building and they could thus spare the expense of the marble.

City Hall has been the scene of many historic events. A gala reception was given here for the Marquis de Lafayette during his triumphal return visit to the United States in 1824. On April 24 and 25, 1865, the body of Abraham Lincoln lay in state in the rotunda under the cupola. In 1927 Lindbergh, returning from his solo flight across the Atlantic, was received on the steps of City Hall by hero-worshipping New Yorkers. The Governor's room inside the building is now a museum containing paintings by Sully, Trumbull and other distinguished artists. Behind City Hall rises the majestic Municipal Building, designed in the Roman Eclectic Style by McKim, Mead and White and completed in 1914. Built to straddle Chambers Street, it incorporates a subway station in its foundations. Its ornate tower, which complements and echos the cupola of City Hall, is crowned by the gilt figure of Civic Fame by Adolph A. Weinman.

18. Chinatown. New York's Chinatown may not be as large as San Francisco's, but its unique atmosphere and exotic establishments make it a perennial favorite with New Yorkers and visitors to the city. Chinese immigration to New York began in the middle of the nineteenth century and increased greatly in the twentieth, especially after the relaxation of immigration laws in 1963. Today there are about 25,000 Chinese living in the area, and the number continues to grow. During the 1970s, when the real-estate market in the rest of New York was suffering a recession, the limited availability of land in Chinatown made prices and rents for stores soar. New housing developments, most notably the federally subsidized Confucius Plaza, have been built to alleviate the district's housing problems. Many of the more prosperous Chinese-Americans are beginning to move to other communities, principally to Queens, but they still return to Chinatown to shop and socialize. Traditionally Chinatown's boundaries have been The Bowery, Mulberry Street and Canal Street, but in the present boom it is gradually extending itself, especially north of Canal Street into Little Italy, causing some friction between the two communities. Within Chinatown there are about 200 restaurants, most of them packed during weekends. They serve the Chinese fare most favored by Americans as well as more authentic dishes such as sea cucumbers, snails and fried jellyfish. The area has several Buddhist temples and various social organizations that form the backbone of the community. There are a large number of shops catering to the tourist trade, as well as garment shops, import-export concerns and some of the best food shops in the city, specializing in Chinese delicacies. This view of Mott Street, looking south across Canal Street, shows the pagoda-like Chinese Merchants Association on the right.

19. Little Italy. Of all the ethnic neighborhoods that add to New York's unique color, Little Italy is perhaps the most famous. It is bounded roughly by Canal Street to the south, Houston Street to the north, The Bowery to the east and Lafayette Street to the west. The area acquired its flavor when many Italians, most of them from the south of Italy, settled there during the great period of immigration from the 1870s through the early years of this century. One of the city's longer-lived ethnic enclaves, Little Italy still flourishes, while other settlements, such as the once thriving Jewish section on the Lower East Side, have dwindled. Although many Italian-Americans of the present generation have moved to the suburbs, Little Italy remains a focal point of many of their social activities. The crowds that fill the streets are warm and gregarious; the feeling of neighborhood is very strong. Specialty shops, a profusion of restaurants, social clubs, pork butchers, sidewalk cafés redolent of espresso, bakeries offering overstuffed cannoli—all make Little Italy a delight to the visitor. In the days around September 18th, the day of Saint Januarius of Naples, Little Italy celebrates the Festa di San Gennaro; Mulberry Street between Canal and Houston Streets is closed to traffic and New York's largest street fair is held. Stands offering a wide variety of native Italian foods and games of chance line the street. There are entertainments and the saint's statue is carried in the traditional procession. The Festa is advertised in the banner hanging over the street in this photograph, taken on Mulberry Street between Hester and Grand Streets. Paolucci's Restaurant (far right) is housed in a building that was constructed in 1816 as the home of Stephen van Rensselaer; the area was first developed after the Revolution as a residential fringe, the heart of the city still being located below Canal Street.

20. Orchard Street. It may lack the elegant shops of Fifth Avenue and the massive department stores of the Herald Square area, but Orchard Street on the Lower East Side packs in crowds during the week and enormous throngs on Sundays. Shoppers are lured by bargains, especially in clothing. Even though the methods are old-world and highly personal, the business transactions involve millions of dollars. The street is one of the few landmarks of the Lower East Side that have survived the urban renewal of the past years. Stores flourish in tenement buildings that once housed the floods of immigrants who came to this country at the close of the last century and the beginning of this one. The immense Jewish community that occupied this neighborhood has dwindled as younger generations have moved to Brooklyn, Queens and the suburbs, but most of the businesses on Orchard Street are still run by Jews, and many of those who moved away still return to shop. The pushcarts that once lined the street were banned by Mayor Fiorello La Guardia in 1939. Those who remember them lament their passing, but are glad that the street still retains so much of its old flavor.

21. The Bowery *(above).* Now internationally famous as New York's skid row, The Bowery (from Dutch *bouwerij,* "farm") originated as an Indian trail, then developed as a lane that ran between the farms of the Dutch colonists. It may well be the oldest street in the United States. In the days of New Amsterdam, it was one of the principal roads leading to the little settlement. Its importance was reinforced when Peter Stuyvesant established his Great Bouwerie and later Bouwerie Village in the general area of today's Astor Place and St. Mark's Place. When the English took over New Amsterdam, they extended the road up to Harlem. It was in use by 1673, and became a part of the Post Road up to Boston. In 1732 the first stage traveled the route to Boston in two weeks. During this period, entertainments made their first association with The Bowery when several genteel taverns opened. The Bowery was then tree-lined and ran through the estates of many of New York's foremost families: the Roosevelts, Beekmans, De Lanceys and De Peysters. The Bowery developed rapidly, and by the time of the Revolution it had many licensed liquor dealers along it—an omen of things to come. During the British occupation of New York, troops were encamped along the road and taverns and places of amusement sprang up to cater to their needs. Commercial pressure from East River shipping was another factor that drove the fashionable world away from The Bowery to Broadway. In 1826 the Bowery Theatre was built just below Canal Street. For many years it was one of the city's most prestigious theaters; artists such as Maria Malibran, Edwin Forrest, Charlotte Cushman and Junius Brutus Booth appeared on its stage. The theater burned several times, but was rebuilt. As a street, however, The Bowery continued its slow decline. By the middle of the nineteenth century it was noted for its crime, "toughs," variety halls and beer gardens. At times its ethnic diversity became explosive. By the turn of the century it had lost most of its flamboyance. What remained were a few bars and flophouses that made the street a mecca for the city's derelicts. Today a change is taking place. The flophouses are still there, but the street is also known as a center for businesses that sell lighting fixtures and kitchen supplies to New York's commercial establishments. In the vicinity of 4th Street, The Bowery is part of the "Rialto of Off-Off-Broadway." Many groups in the neighborhood, especially the LaMama Experimental Theatre Club, have become a vital part of the city's cultural life. Artists and writers have begun to explore The Bowery as a place to set up studios and apartments. Phebe's Place, at No. 361 The Bowery, is one of their favorite meeting spots.

22. Lower Broadway *(opposite).* Although modern businesses thrive along Broadway between Canal and 14th Streets, much of the architecture and feel of the street are firmly rooted in the nineteenth century. Very early in the century the street was fashionably residential; a survivor of the type of house that was to be found there is the Old Merchant's House, 29 East 4th Street. But by the 1850s Broadway had developed as the main commercial thoroughfare of the city. Along the wide sidewalks were built many of New York's most important stores (connecting with the Grand Street shopping district), hotels, theaters and business offices. Such large emporiums as Arnold Constable's, Tiffany's and Lord & Taylor were located here before moving farther uptown. Many of the commercial structures were built with cast-iron facades, an attractive and striking method of construction that prefigured the modern "steel curtain." A large number survive, and are incorporated into the Cast-Iron Historic District. One of the earliest and most beautiful is John P. Gaynor's Haughwout Building at the northeast corner of Broadway and Broome Street. Opened in 1857 its design was inspired by the Sansovino Library in Venice. So successful was it that many of the later cast-iron buildings reflect a Venetian influence. Toward the end of the century the popularity of cast iron waned, and many of the subsequent loft buildings that rise along Broadway were built with stone and brick facades. The street has been spared massive redevelopment, so that a stroll along it is a walk through 75 years of the city's commercial history.

23. SoHo *(above).* The area known today as SoHo (an abbreviation of its location, *S*outh of *Ho*uston Street) is roughly bounded by Canal Street to the south, Houston Street to the north, West Broadway to the west and Crosby Street to the east. The area first began to develop early in the nineteenth century, when the marshy land that separated it from the developed portion of the city was drained. In the first quarter of the century Broadway, the major artery of the district, developed as an exclusive residential neighborhood, but as it grew in commercial importance toward the middle of the century, its desirability as a residential area declined and a considerable number of freed slaves moved in. The entertainment district shifted there from The Bowery and a notorious red-light district flourished around Broadway and Greene Street. The area enjoyed its heyday in the 1860s but was in a decline by 1900, and in the present century its loft buildings were used primarily by light industry. Then, in the 1960s, artists began to take advantage of the low rents and large lofts by setting up their studios there, even though this was in violation of zoning regulations. The city changed its ordinances to encourage them, and today the neighborhood has an international reputation as a vital part of New York's art scene. Many galleries have opened there, as well as restaurants and crafts shops. It is ironical to note that many of the artists who pioneered this change in SoHo have since been driven out by the rise in rents as the area has become more fashionable. This view shows Spring Street looking west toward West Broadway.

24. Shakespeare Festival Public Theatre, Lafayette Street near Astor Place *(opposite).* The building that now houses one of

New York's most dynamic theatrical institutions started life in 1849 as a library. Construction was begun with funds allocated in the will of John Jacob Astor. The city's first free library, it was constructed in the Italianate style in three stages. The south wing, by Alexander Saeltzer, was completed in 1853; the central section, by Griffith Thomas, was finished in 1859; and the north wing, by Thomas Stent, was completed in 1881. Patrons of the Astor Library included Washington Irving and William Makepeace Thackeray. The library vacated the premises in 1912, when the collection was merged with the Lenox Library and the Tilden Foundation to form the nucleus of the New York Public Library at 42nd Street and Fifth Avenue (No. 43). The Hebrew Immigrant Aid Society later took possession of the building, and remained there until 1965. Just as this society was about to sell the property for half a million dollars, the city's Landmarks Preservation Commission, in its first meeting, declared the structure a landmark. Joseph Papp, the energetic producer of the New York Shakespeare Festival, heard of the building's availability and raised the money to purchase it. Brilliantly converted into several theaters of various sizes by Giorgio Cavaglieri, the building was opened to the public in 1967. Since then many daring and original works have been presented there, developing many new talents in the process. *A Chorus Line*, the record-breaking musical, was developed and premiered at the Public Theatre before it was moved uptown to Broadway. The whole enterprise demonstrates how worthwhile buildings can be "recycled" to meet modern needs without damaging their original beauty.

25. Cooper Union, Astor Place. Foundation Hall of Cooper Union is one of the nation's most significant buildings, both historically and architecturally. The school, which specializes in humanities, architecture and fine arts, was endowed by Peter Cooper (1791–1883), a remarkable inventor, industrialist and philanthropist. He built America's first successful railway locomotive, the *Tom Thumb*, helped Samuel F. B. Morse develop the telegraph and aided in the laying of the first Atlantic cable. He was also instrumental in developing America's iron industry. Steel railway rails produced at his mill in Trenton were used to form the building's framework; this was the first time that steel was so employed. In this respect the building is a direct ancestor of Manhattan's famed skyscrapers. Designed in the Italianate style by Frederic A. Peterson, it was opened in 1859. The floors above the cornice that bears the name "Cooper Union" were later additions. The "stovepipe" on the roof marks the termination of the building's elevator shaft; although a practical elevator had not yet been developed, Cooper anticipated it and had the shaft included in the original design. Within the building is the Great Hall, an auditorium with many historical associations. It was there, on February 27, 1860, that Abraham Lincoln delivered the "might makes right" speech that established him as the leading Republican candidate for the Presidency. Subsequently, every President down to Wilson spoke there. Since its opening, the school has maintained a policy of free admissions; to gain entrance, however, applicants must pass rigorous examinations. The school has expanded to several buildings, and the Foundation Building has been given a complete renovation.

26. Grace Church, 10th Street and Broadway. Grace Episcopal Church is generally regarded as one of the finest examples of Gothic Revival architecture in the city and the nation. Yet its architect, James Renwick, had never seen a Gothic building at first hand when, at the age of 25, he designed the structure in 1843. He received most of his inspiration from books containing the designs of Augustus W. Pugin. Constructed of white marble quarried at Sing Sing, the church was opened in 1846. In the nineteenth century it housed one of the most fashionable congregations in New York. For many years sexton Isaac Hull Brown took care of the needs not only of the church, but of New York society as well, becoming an arbiter in such matters as drawing up guest lists. While many brilliant weddings were held in the church, the most famous was probably also the strangest. On January 10, 1863, Charles Sherwood Stratton (better known as P. T. Barnum's star attraction, General Tom Thumb) married Lavinia Warren Bumpus, also a midget. In 1888 two adjacent buildings designed by Renwick's firm were completed, 1806 Broadway and Grace Church School. Executed in the Gothic Revival Style like the church, they preserved the architectural integrity of the complex. The view of Grace Church from points below it on Broadway is striking; it stands precisely where the street bends to the west as it heads north, and is thus at the center of the vista. A story told by New Yorkers holds that the street turns here because of farmer Hendrick Brevoort. According to the legend, when the city fathers were extending Broadway uptown, they wanted to continue it in a straight line which would have cut through Brevoort's beloved apple orchard. Brevoort, who was something of a curmudgeon, stood in front of his property with a blunderbuss, and the street was scared off to the side.

27. Washington Square Park. Washington Square Park was originally a marsh, through which ran Minetta Brook (now completely covered over). At the end of the eighteenth century and the beginning of the nineteenth, the land was used as a potter's field and the site of public executions; when the park underwent renovations in 1970, the bones of thousands of early New Yorkers were unearthed. In 1826 the land became the Washington Military Parade Ground and a public park. The park became extremely fashionable, and in the 1830s was built the distinguished row of Greek Revival mansions that still stands on Washington Square North. Henry James's maternal grandmother, Elizabeth Walsh, lived in No. 18 (demolished). In later years he used the house as the setting for his novel *Washington Square*, subsequently adapted for stage and screen as *The Heiress.* Later in the century, when the nouveaux riches made their home in imitation French châteaux on upper Fifth Avenue, the Row remained the bastion of old Knickerbocker society. The Washington Memorial Arch, featured in the photo, is one of the most famous in the world. Dedicated in 1895, it was designed by Stanford White to replace a temporary arch that had been built at Fifth Avenue and 8th Street in 1889 to commemorate the centenary of Washington's inauguration. The reliefs on the arch are the work of Frederick MacMonnies; the statues on the piers facing north are *Washington in War* by Hermon A. MacNeil and *Washington in Peace* by A. Stirling Calder. Beyond the arch rise the prestigious luxury apartment houses of lower Fifth Avenue. The park is greatly valued as one of the few large open spaces in Greenwich Village. On warm, fine weekends and holidays it is packed with crowds strolling, playing games and listening to musicians and soapbox orators.

28. New York University, Washington Square (*above*). One of the world's largest private institutions of learning, New York University has been located around Washington Square since it was founded in 1831 by Albert Gallatin, Jefferson's Secretary of State. In 1837 its main building, a Gothic Revival structure influenced by King's College Chapel of Cambridge University, rose on the square. Prison labor was used in constructing the building; this angered the stone masons of the city, who rioted so violently that the National Guard had to be called in. It was in the main building that, in 1839, Professor John Draper, while experimenting with the process newly developed by Daguerre in France, took what was probably the first photographic portrait. While an instructor of painting at the college, Samuel F. B. Morse developed the telegraph. Walt Whitman taught poetry there, Samuel Colt invented the six-shooter there and Winslow Homer painted in one of its studios. The building was demolished in 1894 to make way for the present Main Building (seen here). Henry James wrote: "The grey and more or less hallowed University Building . . . has vanished from the earth, and vanished with it the two or three adjacent houses, of which my birth place was one." Since then the university has grown to include 15 colleges, as well as the graduate programs, increasing in size until it now owns almost all the land around the square. Many object that some of the new university buildings, notably the Holy Trinity Chapel and monolithic Bobst Library on Washington Square South, have destroyed the former harmony of the square. At the same time the university, through its ownership, has salvaged many of the houses along the Row on Washington Square North, as well as Washington Mews. The statue of

Giuseppe Garibaldi (right), by Giovanni Turini, was erected in 1888 through the auspices of the Italian-American community. According to a legend beloved to NYU students, the Italian liberator will unsheathe his sword in a salute only when a virgin passes in front of him.

29. Greenwich Village (*opposite*). Many New Yorkers go to Greenwich Village to enjoy its nightlife, but much of the charm for which it is famous is attributable to its great variety of architecture. No other area in New York has preserved so many representative examples of the many different styles that have enjoyed a vogue in the city. A typical block in the Village may have a dormered house of the 1830s standing next to a Romanesque Revival building of the 1880s, a Greek Revival town house of the 1840s or an elegant apartment house of the 1930s; the stretch of Bedford Street between Seventh Avenue South and Commerce Street evokes the dignified simplicity of the earliest years of the Republic. Shown in the photo is St. Luke's Place. Its buildings, in the Italianate style of the 1850s, serve as a reminder of one of the city's most opulent periods. The quiet charm of the street makes it popular with filmmakers for location shots; exteriors for *Wait Until Dark* were taken there. Among the famous who have lived on the street are poet Marianne Moore, painter Paul Cadmus, authors Theodore Dreiser and Sherwood Anderson and sculptor Theodore Roszak. The house in the distance with lamps painted white on the newel post was once the residence of Jimmy Walker, New York's exuberant (and shady) mayor from 1926 to 1933. The custom of installing lamps in front of a mayor's house is said to date from Dutch days.

30. East Village (above). The East Village is bounded, roughly, by The Bowery and Fourth Avenue to the west, 14th Street to the north, the East River to the east and 4th Street to the south. Its development as part of the city began in the 1830s, when the area around Astor Place became a fashionable residential section. Later in the century, business and light industry moved in, and thousands of the immigrants who poured into New York from Europe were jammed into tenements that lined the streets. The neighborhood still reflects the various elements of its history. Elegant Federal and Greek Revival houses are still to be found there, as well as buildings erected by the immigrant German population in the nineteenth century. Some are in an excellent state of preservation; others have been sadly disfigured and neglected. A large Ukrainian community flourishes in the East Village. Second Avenue can no longer be called the Jewish Rialto, as it was at the turn of the century, when several Yiddish theaters operated there, but there is still a Jewish holdover. The population, however, is increasingly Hispanic. During the late 1950s and into the 1960s, the painters and writers who were being forced out of their Greenwich Village studios by rising rents started to move into the East Village, where rents were, and remain, low. It was then that the name East Village was coined by real-estate interests to add to the attractiveness of the area, which had previously been regarded simply as part of the Lower East Side. In the mid-'60s, St. Mark's Place (seen here between Third and Second Avenues) was a magnet for hippies and flower children. The streets were suddenly filled with businesses dealing with the "counterculture" — head shops, organic health-food restaurants and such places of entertainment as Fillmore East. The hippies are gone now and the neighborhood has settled down somewhat, but it re-tains its lively mix of ethnic cultures and social groups.

31. St. Mark's-in-the-Bowery, Second Avenue and 10th Street (opposite). In 1651 Dutch governor Peter Stuyvesant was given a *bouwerie*, or farm, in the area of today's East Village. This he developed into his Great Bouwerie, building a large house on today's Stuyvesant Place. The farm was prosperous, and a small village grew up around it. In 1860 he erected a chapel on the property and dedicated it to Saint Nicholas. When the English took over the city in 1664 (the articles of surrender being arranged at Stuyvesant's house), the crusty former governor withdrew into retirement. He died in 1672, at the age of 80, and was interred in the chapel's crypt. (Stuyvesants continued to be buried there for six generations; the last direct descendant of Peter was Augustus Van Horne Stuyvesant, Jr., who died in 1953.) After the chapel was taken down in 1793, Petrus Stuyvesant, Peter's great-grandson, offered Trinity Parish the land and 800 pounds if it would construct a church on the site. The offer was accepted and Saint Mark's was completed in 1799. The steeple, added in 1828, was designed by Ithiel Town, who was one of the leading proponents of the Greek Revival Style. The Italianate cast-iron portico was erected in 1854, making the church a curious, yet harmonious, amalgam of styles. A blaze gutted the interior in 1978, but restoration was begun immediately. The years have also seen a dramatic change in the church's congregation; once prosperous and middle-class, it is now comprised mainly of the less well-to-do. The church has adapted to the changing needs of its congregation, and has for some time been marked by its progressive attitude on religious and social matters. The bust of Peter Stuyvesant outside the church was the gift of Queen Wilhelmina of the Netherlands.

32

32. 14th Street. It may now look a bit down at the heel, but 14th Street has a colorful past. It began life in the 1830s, when Union Square was opened and the surrounding area became a prime residential neighborhood; the only structure that survives intact from that era is the Norwood House, 241 West 14th Street. Things change quickly in New York, and by the Civil War the street had begun to take on a commercial character. In 1854 the Academy of Music, the first opera house in New York to stage seasons of opera successfully, was opened with a performance of *Norma*. The house prospered until it lost out in competition with the Metropolitan Opera, which opened uptown in 1883 (see No. 69); thereafter it became a regular theater showing mixed attractions. In 1926 it fell to the wrecker's ball, along with old Tammany Hall, seat of the powerful Democratic political organization, and Tony Pastor's Variety Theatre; on the site was built the Consolidated Edison Building with its imposing tower. Further connections with classical music on 14th Street were the piano showrooms that opened in the neighborhood and Steinway Hall, where recitals were given. Other theaters were opened on the street, which, in the '70s and '80s, flourished as the city's theatrical center. In the '80s and '90s this center moved up to Madison Square and to Herald Square, and finally settled around Times Square in the early years of the present century. Restaurants also flourished in the area. Lüchow's Restaurant, opened in 1882, dated from the time when it stood in the midst of a thriving German community. Caruso dined there, as did Lillian Russell, "Diamond" Jim Brady and Victor Herbert. As a shopping center the 14th Street area enjoyed its heyday in the 1880s and '90s. R. H. Macy had his store there (part still survives at 56 West 14th), as did Tiffany and Brentano's, as well as some concerns, such as James A. Hearn & Son (34-40 West 14th) and Baumann Brothers (22 East 14th), that are now remembered by only a few. Over the years the street declined into a bargain shopping district. Most famous of the bargain emporiums was S. Klein's. The street has assumed a distinctly Hispanic note. The many bargain stores display merchandise along the sidewalk, creating a bazaar-like atmosphere. The Salvation Army has its headquarters at 136 West 14th, adding a sober touch.

33. Union Square. When New York's grid plan was laid out in 1811, the intersection of Fourth Avenue and Broadway was named Union Place. The present park, developed in 1831 by Samuel B. Ruggles, also responsible for Gramercy Park, was soon surrounded by the houses of the wealthy. The commercial world took over the area after the Civil War, and at the end of the First World War the whole park was elevated a few feet to make room for the subway station that was constructed beneath it. Union Square has long been a rallying point in the city. Troops paraded here during the Civil War. In the 1870s Tammany Hall, the powerful Democratic organization, held torchlight rallies here. As the labor movement gained strength in the 1880s, it held protest marches around the park, which remains the traditional place for workers' May Day celebrations. Union Square was also the site of meetings protesting the executions of Sacco and Vanzetti and the Rosenbergs. Like those at Speaker's Corner in London's Hyde Park, the park's soapbox orators direct their tirades at the public. The park also contains several noteworthy pieces of statuary. Most important is Henry Kirke Brown's equestrian statue of George Washington, shown here. Unveiled in 1856, it was the first major public sculpture erected in New York after the Revolution, and it started a craze for public statuary that continued well into this century. The work depicts Washington entering New York in 1783 on Evacuation Day, when the British finally withdrew their forces from the city. A statue of Lincoln (1866) is also by Brown. Near Fourth Avenue is a statue of Lafayette (1876) by Frédéric-Auguste Bartholdi, most famous for the Statue of Liberty (No. 4).

34. Gramercy Park. While most neighborhoods of New York City have experienced dramatic changes during their history, Gramercy Park has remained fashionable and exclusive ever since Samuel B. Ruggles created a brilliant real-estate development by purchasing and draining the swampy land in 1831. On it he created a 1½-acre park surrounded by building lots. Buyers of the plots were entitled to keys to the park, an arrangement common in the beginning of the nineteenth century, and one that continues in Gramercy Park to this day (other squares that operated under this arrangement have either been opened to the public or have simply disappeared). Some of the most charming architecture in New York lines the park. The ornate cast-iron porches and balconies of Nos. 3, 4 and 5 Gramercy Park West (1846) are thought to be the work of Alexander Jackson Davis. The Players Club (No. 16 Gramercy Park South) was originally the home of the great American actor Edwin Booth. It was given to the Players in 1888, when it was remodeled by Stanford White. The private club counts among its members some of the most distinguished people in the arts and letters. The elaborate (and badly weathered) brownstone National Arts Club, No. 15 Gramercy Park South, was built by Calvert Vaux in 1874. The statue of *Edwin Booth in the Character of Hamlet* stands in the center of the park; sculptured by Edmond T. Quinn, it was unveiled in 1916. More important than any one particular aspect is the atmosphere of the square, elegant and serene, reminiscent of the many residential squares of London.

35. Bellevue Hospital Center, First Avenue between 26th and 30th Streets. The oldest public hospital in the United States and the largest municipal hospital in Manhattan, Bellevue is renowned for the excellence and scope of its facilities. With the addition of the new 25-story patient-care building (the large square building in the center of the photograph), it now stretches along First Avenue from 26th to 30th Streets and east to the Franklin D. Roosevelt Drive. Bellevue can trace its origin back to 1736, when it functioned as an infirmary in New York City's first almshouse. It was moved to its present site soon after the War of 1812 and took the name of Bellevue Hospital in 1825. Since then its growth has been rapid. Many of its buildings erected in the beginning of the century were designed by McKim, Mead and White. From its earliest years the hospital has pioneered many innovations. The first instruction in anatomy by actual dissection recorded in the United States occurred there in 1750. The hypodermic syringe was first administered there in 1856. In 1867 Bellevue established the first outpatient clinic in the country. Two years later it set up the world's first hospital-based ambulance service. Clinical teaching was begun in 1847, and today the New York University School of Medicine has full responsibility for the hospital's clinical services. Students are eager to receive training at Bellevue, for the hospital claims that there is almost no disease known to man that is not treated there. It is especially noted for its psychiatric hospital and treatment of patients with chronic diseases of the chest. Each year more than 25,000 patients are admitted to Bellevue. It has nearly 100 outpatient clinics which service 500,000 annually. Seen in the photo behind the new building is the new Waterside Housing complex on the East River, one of several new developments to capitalize on the city's extensive waterfront for residential purposes.

36. Flatiron Building, Fifth Avenue and 23rd Street *(opposite)*. Built for the Fuller Construction Company and opened in 1902, the three-sided 20-story structure was quickly dubbed the Flatiron Building from its resemblance to the household appliance. It is the work of the distinguished Chicago-based architect Daniel H. Burnham, a leading light of the influential Columbian Exposition of 1893. An early skyscraper, the Flatiron Building is supported by a steel framework; its elaborate limestone Renaissance Eclectic facade is simply a dressing. When it originally rose on the triangular plot — "the cowcatcher" — bounded by 22nd Street and the crossing of Fifth Avenue and Broadway at 23rd Street, New Yorkers held their breath waiting for "Burnham's Folly" to topple over in the first strong wind. The corner can be one of the windiest in the city when gusts blowing down Fifth Avenue and Broadway and across Madison Square Park merge. Men gathered at the 23rd Street corner of the building to watch the winds lift the skirts of passing beauties, affording forbidden glimpses of ankle. A New York legend holds that it was the action of policemen quickly moving the loiterers on that gave rise to the expression "give them the twenty-three skidoo." On the right is the Toy Center, office of most of New York's manufacturers and distributors in the toy trade. It stands on the site of the Fifth Avenue Hotel, one of the most fashionable hotels during the last half of the nineteenth century. Looking down Broadway and Fifth Avenue at this point, one sees many of the handsome commercial buildings of 50 years ago, when this was the fashionable center of business and shopping.

37. Madison Square *(above)*. In its natural state, Madison Square was swampland. Like Washington Square, it was first used as a potter's field. When the grid plan, establishing the

city's present arrangement in rectangular blocks, was laid out in 1811, provision was made for a parade ground bounded by Third and Seventh Avenues and by 23rd and 34th Streets. Over the years its size was reduced. By the middle of the century the park had been fixed at its present size. The fashionable world moved up around the square; the home of Leonard Jerome, maternal grandfather of Winston Churchill, stood there until recently. Many of New York's smartest hotels, including the Fifth Avenue Hotel, the Brunswick and the Hoffman House, attracted a wealthy and illustrious clientele. At the legendary Delmonico's one dined in luxury. As the century drew to a close, the area around the square became a focus of New York's nightlife. In 1890, Stanford White's Madison Square Garden was opened at Madison Avenue and 26th Street. Ironically, the brilliant architect was shot to death there in 1906. In 1893 the Metropolitan Life Insurance Company began to build on the east side of the square; the building went up in stages, and the entire complex was not finished until 1950. This incursion of the business community was followed in 1902 by the Flatiron Building and, bit by bit, the more fashionable and lively elements that had clustered around the square moved north. The park itself, a welcome bit of greenery in midtown Manhattan, has some interesting works of sculpture. By far the most important is Augustus Saint-Gaudens' statue of Admiral Farragut (1880). The base, designed by the ill-fated White, complements the nautical theme of the work, and is a prefiguration of Art Nouveau. The statue of Roscoe Conkling by John Q. A. Ward (1893) marks the spot where the notorious politician collapsed from exhaustion during the Blizzard of 1888. Although rescued, he died six weeks later.

38. Episcopal Church of the Transfiguration (Little Church Around the Corner), 29th Street East of Fifth Avenue *(above).* It was 1870. Actor George Holland had died and his friend, the famous Joseph Jefferson, went to a fashionable church near here to arrange for the burial. When the pastor learned that the deceased had been on the "disreputable" stage, he refused to perform the service. With distaste, he directed Jefferson to "the little church around the corner." Jefferson went there and found himself welcome. Since that time there has been a close bond between the church and the acting profession, including John Drew, Edwin Booth, Otis Skinner, George Arliss, Sarah Bernhardt, Sir Henry Irving and many others. The church itself was built in 1849–56 to the plans of an unknown architect. The city's only example of the fourteenth-century Cottage Gothic style, the church has a tower that stands in vivid contrast to the Art Deco Empire State Building, which rises behind it. The church is approached through a lich gate (used in the early part of some burial services, before the body is brought into the church); this was designed by Frederick Withers in 1896. The church has always taken an active role in the community. During the draft riots that devastated the city in 1863, it harbored Blacks, saving them from lynching and murder at the hands of crazed mobs. In the Great Depression the church operated a soup kitchen that helped keep many New Yorkers alive.

39. Empire State Building, Fifth Avenue and 34th Street *(opposite).* The Empire State Building, rising 1,472 feet above Fifth Avenue and 34th Street, has become a symbol of New York City. Until the World Trade Center briefly claimed the distinction, it was the tallest building in the world. Each year nearly two million visitors crowd the observatories on the 86th and 102nd floors to enjoy an unparalleled view, extending for 80 miles in good weather. The 222-foot-tall television transmission antenna, serving nine stations in the metropolitan area, was built in 1950. Sixty-seven high-speed passenger elevators whisk some 16,000 employees to the offices of more than 900 firms in the building, which serves as the New York headquarters for such industries as footwear, man-made fiber, men's wear, notions and women's hosiery. At night, the upper 30 stories are brilliantly illuminated; during the migration season, in cooperation with the National Audubon Society, the lights are turned off in order not to disorient the birds, which might otherwise fly into the building. The Empire State Building stands on the site of the old Astor Mansion. It was the capacity of Mrs. William Astor's ballroom in this house that determined the famous "Four Hundred" of New York society's elite at the turn of the century. The mansion was eventually razed, and on the site the Waldorf-Astoria was erected. When the hotel decided to move to its present location on Park Avenue (see No. 59), New York was enjoying a boom in skyscraper construction and the idea of creating the mammoth Empire State came into being. Designed by Shreve, Lamb & Harmon Associates in a pure Art Deco style, it was opened on May 1, 1931. During the Depression, the building had few occupants and was only able to maintain itself through the fees it collected from visitors to the observatories. A dirigible mooring was built at what is now the base of the television tower, but it was never used; a single attempt nearly ended in disaster. The building also managed to withstand the impact of a B-25 bomber that hit the 79th floor in 1945. Miraculously, only seven people were killed. Finally, in the minds of millions of moviegoers the Empire State Building is forever associated with the spectacular finale of the 1933 *King Kong.*

40. Macy's, Herald Square. The Herald Square area is one of the city's largest shopping districts, and Macy's, self-proclaimed as the world's largest store, is probably the most famous of its stores. Macy's has been in operation in New York since 1858, when Roland Husey Macy opened a small store on Sixth Avenue (his three previous ventures as a merchant had proven unsuccessful). The business prospered and grew. The Broadway Building (seen in the photo) was opened in 1902. Its Beaux-Arts facade is the work of architects De Lemos & Cordes. When the company was acquiring the land for the building, it was able to buy all the plots it needed with the exception of the one at the corner of Broadway and 34th Street. The house that stood there had been purchased by Robert Smith, who owned a business that competed with Macy's. He refused to sell the land and Macy's had to build around it. The house is covered by the huge sign seen in the photo. It is said that the department store used to pay a huge amount to rent the space. In the 1920s and 1930s the store expanded until it took up the entire block bounded by 34th and 35th Streets and by Broadway and Seventh Avenue, save for the small southeast corner lot. Each day over 150,000 people shop in the store's two million square feet of selling space, and are served by about 11,000 employees. The Herald Square area was the city's tenderloin in the 1870s; in the last part of the nineteenth century it housed the theater district, which had steadily been moving uptown. The McKim, Mead and White building erected in 1895 for the *New York Herald* stood on the Square, giving it its name. The little triangular park at the north end of the square incorporates two owls, the figure of Minerva and the two bellringers (nicknamed Stuff and Guff) that stood on the building until it was demolished in 1921.

41. Madison Square Garden, Eighth Avenue and 34th Street.
Each year over five million spectators flock to the great variety of attractions offered at Madison Square Garden. The indoor arena has a flexible seating capacity, accommodating a maximum of about 20,000. Depending on what night you go, you may see the National Horse Show, a wrestling or boxing match, the pageantry of the Ringling Brothers Barnum & Bailey Circus, the Knickerbockers playing basketball, an ice show, the Rangers playing hockey, or a rock concert. In 1976 the Democratic National Convention that met here nominated Jimmy Carter as its Presidential candidate. The building also houses the Felt Forum, an amphitheater seating 5,050 which is used for smaller-scale attractions. The 64,000-square-foot Exposition Rotunda is used for a variety of purposes that do not require seating, such as animal shows, the National Antiques Show and the National Postage Stamp Show. The present Garden, built by Charles Luckman Associates at a cost of $60 million, was opened February 11,

1968 with a U.S.O. Benefit starring Bob Hope, Bing Crosby and Rocky Marciano. It is the fourth structure to bear the name. The first, at Madison Avenue and 26st Street near Madison Square, started life as a railway depot; it became P. T. Barnum's Hippodrome in 1874, later Gilmore's Garden, and was named Madison Square Garden in 1879. The second Garden, designed by Stanford White, opened on the same site in 1890. The Democratic National Convention held there in 1924 balloted 104 times before nominating John W. Davis, who lost to Calvin Coolidge. That structure was never economical to operate, and in 1925 the Garden moved to a building at Eighth Avenue between 49th and 50th Streets (subsequently demolished). The present Garden stands on the site of McKim, Mead and White's monumental Pennsylvania Station, demolished in the 1960s. The trains still operate beneath the complex, but in surroundings considerably less grand than they used to be.

42. Pierpont Morgan Library, 36th Street and Madison Avenue. Pierpont Morgan inherited two things from his father Junius: a vast fortune and a passion for collecting. By the turn of the century his collection of books, incunabula, manuscripts and works of art had grown so large that he hired the firm of McKim, Mead, and White to build a library near his mansion, which still stands on the southeast corner of Madison Avenue and 37th Street. The building, personally designed by Charles McKim in the Italian Renaissance style, and completed in 1906, is undoubtedly one of the finest pieces of architecture in New York. The white marble of the exterior is "fitted"; the stones were cut so exactly that no mortar was needed to join them; it is impossible to slip a penknife into the joins. Such a feat could only have been accomplished in an era when an enormous supply of money and highly skilled craftsmen were available. When Morgan died in 1913 the collection was opened to the public. In 1924 it was incorporated as a public library, and four years later an annex, designed by Benjamin W. Morris and including a new principal entrance, was added to the west. Most of the splendid interior remains as it was during Morgan's lifetime. It was in the opulent setting of the West Room that he gathered prominent financiers on November 2, 1907, to stem the panic caused by the collapse of the Knickerbocker Trust Co. Drawing upon its collections and on superb loan material, the library mounts rare and beautiful exhibitions for the general public and provides an invaluable resource for scholars. Highlights of the collection include Gutenberg Bibles, Caxton first editions, the original manuscript of Dickens' *A Christmas Carol*, medieval and Renaissance illuminated manuscripts, Babylonian seals, autographs and Rembrandt etchings.

43. New York Public Library, Fifth Avenue and 42nd Street.
Designed by the prestigious firm of Carrère & Hastings, the New York Public Library is one of America's greatest Beaux-Arts buildings. The land on which it stands was used as a potter's field at the beginning of the nineteenth century. In 1843 the Croton Reservoir, contained by massive walls in the Neo-Egyptian style, was completed on the site. In 1899 the construction of the Croton Dam in northern Westchester County eliminated the need for the reservoir. It was demolished in 1900 to make way for the library, which was inaugurated in 1911. It was the money of Andrew Carnegie, over five million dollars, that subsidized most of the building's construction. The core of the collection was formed by the consolidation of the Astor Library, the Lenox Library and the Tilden Trust. The names of these sources are inscribed over the main entrance, flanked by Paul Bartlett's statues representing (from left to right) Philosophy, Romance, Religion, Poetry, Drama and History. The famous pair of lions by Edward C. Potter (only one of which is visible here) are reminiscent of Landseer's lions at the base of Nelson's Column in Trafalgar Square. Potter's lions were recently cleaned and treated to make them resistant to the erosive quality of New York's air. The main lobby of the building is one of New York's most regal interior spaces and, along with the exterior, has been designated a landmark. The collection within the building is comprised of over four million books. Among the library's many divisons are: manuscripts and rare books; maps; prints; science and technology; art and architecture; American history and genealogy. With its enormous main reading room for the basic reference collection, the library is a priceless resource for scholars and students the world over.

44. Grand Central Terminal, 42nd Street and Park Avenue
(opposite). This is the second station to stand on the site. The
first, a cast-iron structure in the Second Empire style, was
erected in 1871 and enlarged in 1899. When steam engines
were banned from the city in 1902, the New York Central
decided that, rather than abandon the city, they would elec-
trify the rails and build a new station. The magnificent
Beaux-Arts structure was designed by architects Whitney
Warren and James Wetmore in close collaboration with
engineers Reed & Stem. The building was completed in 1913;
the roadway that runs around it was added in 1919. Over the
entrance is the monumental group *Transportation* by Jules-
Alexis Coutan. Mercury stands in the center; on the left is
Hercules; on the right, Minerva. Directly below stands a
statue of Commodore Vanderbilt, who had had the first station constructed. The main concourse of the building is huge.
The ceiling, painted blue and picked out with lights to represent the constellations, is about ten stories above the floor.
The windows alone are 75 feet tall. The great days of the
long-distance trains such as the Twentieth Century Limited
are now over, but thousands of commuters pour through the
station each day, coming from the Westchester and Connec-
ticut communities. Although the station has been declared a
landmark, it has recently been threatened by various schemes
to put its site to more profitable use. Concerned New Yorkers
are fighting to save it from the fate of McKim, Mead and
White's Pennsylvania Station, which was leveled in 1963–66.
Grand Central remains a great entrance to a great city.
45. Pan Am Building, Park Avenue and 44th Street *(above).* Of
all of New York's many skyscrapers, the Pan Am Building,
erected in 1963, is one of the most conspicuous and least
liked. Objections are not so much against the building itself, a
52-story block with over two million square feet of office
space, as to its location on this particular site. Formerly,
views along Park Avenue were dominated by the New York
Central Building (from the north) and by Grand Central Station (from the south). Both views were equally pleasing. Upon
publication of plans for the Pan Am Building, designed by
Walter Gropius, Emery Roth & Sons and Pietro Belluschi,
New Yorkers protested against the way the new building
would destroy the sense of scale on Park Avenue. How right
they were can be judged from this photograph, in which
Grand Central is dwarfed by the building. A heliport was
constructed atop the tower, from which helicopters were to
whisk businessmen to the New York airports; but public op-
position to it was great. After a temporary disruption, service
was resumed in 1977, only to be discontinued soon after
when a helicopter tipped over on the pad. Passengers were
killed and debris falling onto the street and into adjacent offices caused additional casualities.

46. Times Square. Although it is no longer the "Crossroads of the World," Times Square still attracts millions every year. The area's earliest historic association of note is with the Revolution: in 1776 Washington met Israel Putnam at the site of 44th Street and Broadway to plan the Battle of Harlem. In the nineteenth century the area was the center of the horse-and-carriage trade. The intersection of Seventh Avenue and Broadway was thus named Long Acre Square, after Long Acre, the carriage district of London. The famous Brewster carriages, some of which are today on display at the New-York Historical Society, were made in a factory at the north end of the square. At the turn of the century the city's theatrical district made its move into the neighborhood. In 1895 Oscar Hammerstein's Olympia, a complex containing two theaters and a roof garden, opened on the block between 44th and 45th Streets, then a disreputable area known as Thieves' Lair. On December 31, 1904, the *New York Times* opened its new tower, designed by Eidlitz & MacKenzie, at the south end of the square. The event was celebrated with a midnight display of fireworks that set a precedent; New Year's celebrations still take place in the Square, as thousands gather to watch the lowering of an illuminated globe from the top of the tower, symbolizing the death of the old year. The *Times* had decided to move uptown from Park Row when the Broadway–Seventh Avenue Subway line opened. At the urg-ing of Adolph Ochs, publisher of the paper, the station at 42nd Street was named Times Square. In the early part of the century the area boasted a brilliant nightlife. Theaters sprouted like mushrooms; the carriage trade packed the lobster palaces such as Rector's and Shanley's, and stopped at hotels such as the Astor and Knickerbocker. In the 1920s world-famous movie palaces were built in the square; many are now gone. Early makers of electric signs soon found that the open vista of the square made it an excellent spot in which to display glittering advertisements. In 1916 the city fathers gave them a zoning dispensation to construct their outsize extravaganzas that turned night into day. Today the glamor has faded, and the square is in transition. The famous Astor Hotel was demolished and in 1969 an office block was erected on the site. The Times Tower itself, now simply called One Times Square, has been tastelessly refaced. The habitués of the square have also changed. Now the middle class only goes there for dinner and the theater. The movie theaters are no longer glamorous; seedy honkytonk attractions are prevalent. Beginning in the 1980s, many buildings fell before the wrecker's ball as new hotels and office buildings arose. Plans continued for the massive redevelopment of 42nd Street. Nevertheless, the district still has a fascination because of its visual excitement and thriving theater life.

47. Theater District. To millions the word "Broadway" means the New York theater district, an area affectionately associated with such luminaries as Eugene O'Neill, Helen Hayes, Lillian Hellman, Ethel Merman, Edward Albee, Norman Bel Geddes, Katharine Cornell, Maxwell Anderson, Stephen Sondheim, Kurt Weill, Lerner and Loewe, Rodgers and Hammerstein and John Barrymore. The area is bounded roughly by Sixth and Eighth Avenues and 41st and 53rd Streets. Its heart is 44th and 45th Streets. New Yorkers have long loved the theater; there was one in operation as early as 1732 at Nassau Street. Over the years the theater district moved north, along with the rest of the city, first along Broadway to 14th Street, then to Madison and Herald Squares. The Metropolitan Opera opened "way uptown" at 39th Street and Broadway in 1883, and in 1893 Charles Frohman

opened the Empire Theatre a block to the north. Over the next 30 years an unprecedented theatrical boom took place, peaking in the 1927–28 season, when 257 productions played in 71 theaters. The Depression, competition from the movies and increased production costs all took a toll; today the Broadway season does not approach the volume of that golden year. But it is still the most vital theater district in the nation, if not the world. Shown in this photograph taken on Shubert Alley, which runs between 44th and 45th Streets, is the Shubert Theatre (designed by Henry B. Herts and opened in 1913) just before curtain time for *A Chorus Line*. The musical originated at Joseph Papp's Shakespeare Festival on Lafayette Place (see No. 24) and was later transferred to Broadway, to become the longest-running musical in American theatrical history.

48. Chrysler Building, Lexington Avenue and 42nd Street *(left, top).* Designed by William Van Alen, the 77-story Chrysler Building is one of the most spirited of the skyscrapers built during the boom of the late '20s. Since its completion in 1930, its Art Deco needle spire has been one of the most prominent features of the New York skyline. Its flamboyant decorations all relate to the automobile industry. The multiarched dome is made of stainless steel held in place by stainless-steel rivets and bolts, so that the gleaming structure cannot tarnish, rust or corrode. The Chrysler Building was erected in unofficial competition with the 40 Wall Tower on Wall Street, each hoping to be the world's tallest building. When the dome of the Chrysler Building was completed, the structure stood 925 feet tall; the architects of 40 Wall Tower assumed the Chrysler Building was finished, so when they reached 925 feet in their own construction, they added an extra two feet, making 40 Wall the taller of the two. But Van Alen had fooled them; the 123-foot spire was then attached to the Chrysler Building, making *it* the taller. Its triumph was short-lived, for a few months later the Empire State Building was completed and claimed the distinction, which it held until the World Trade Center (see No. 13) was built. Few of the high rises built today loom as tall as the buildings of the '20s and '30s. Construction and maintenance costs have risen astronomically, building regulations are stricter, and the elevator cores of such buildings eat up too much rentable space. In the foreground of the photo is Jules-Alexis Coutan's group *Transportation* on Grand Central Station (see No. 44).

49. Ford Foundation Headquarters, 42nd Street between First and Second Avenues *(left, bottom).* For more than 40 years the Ford Foundation has played a vital role in the economic, political, social and cultural life of the nation. Its mammoth resources are founded on the philanthropic donations of Henry Ford. At the end of the '60s the foundation had assets of over three billion dollars and gave millions of dollars a month in grants for education, international and national affairs, communications, and the arts. Its headquarters, built in 1967 from designs by Kevin Roche, John Dinkeloo & Associates, is one of the pioneer buildings featuring a multistoried roofed atrium. Because of its elegance, its proportions and the quality of its plantings, it has exerted influence on buildings around the world.

50. United Nations, First Avenue between 42nd and 48th Streets *(opposite).* In 1945, at the end of the Second World War, the United Nations Charter was signed in San Francisco, and the organization, devoted to international peace and understanding, was created. Later that year the United States invited the organization to set up its headquarters in this country. In 1946 New York was chosen as host city. A generous gift by John D. Rockefeller, Jr., enabled the organization to purchase its site along the East River, then a rundown area of slaughterhouses and light industries. An international committee of architects, headed by Wallace K. Harrison and including such distinguished members as Le Corbusier and Oscar Niemeyer, designed the complex. (While it was under construction, the United Nations sat at the New York City Building in Flushing Meadows, Queens, originally built for the 1939 World's Fair, and at Lake Success in Nassau County.) The complex is dominated by the 550-foot-tall Secretariat Building, which provides office space. In front is the gently sloping roof of the General Assembly Building. The imposing General Assembly Hall has seating accommodations for the delegates of the 159 member countries and their alternates. Behind the Secretariat is the Conference Building, where the Security Council, the Trusteeship Council and the Economic and Social Council

meet. In 1961 the Dag Hammarskjold Library was dedicated in memory of the Secretary-General who died in Africa while on a peacekeeping mission. Not only does the United Nations have major regulatory bodies, but it also runs many smaller organizations which concern themselves with matters as diverse as atomic energy, international finance and trade, world health, international communications and meteorol-

ogy. The buildings and grounds are enhanced by many works of art donated by member nations. Technically, the property on which the United Nations stands is international and not subject to the jurisdiction of municipal, state or federal governments. Guided tours are given frequently during the day.

51. Fifth Avenue *(above).* Fifth Avenue first attained fame for the mansions that lined it near Washington Square, and lower Fifth Avenue retains this residential quality. From 14th to 34th Streets it is an area of office buildings, many of them unaltered above the first story for the past 50 years. From 34th to 59th Street it is one of the world's great shopping streets, comparable to London's Regent Street or Paris's Rue de Rivoli. To 110th Street it is again mainly luxury-residential, but above 110th Street its character changes completely as it runs through Harlem. The shopping district, seen here, is lined with many of the nation's most exclusive stores. One can buy fabulously expensive jewelry at Cartier's (housed in a converted 1905 mansion of a type that once flourished in the neighborhood), Tiffany's or Harry Winston, Inc. The casual stroller can enjoy the ingenious window displays created by these establishments. For clothing there are stores such as Bergdorf-Goodman, Saks Fifth Avenue and Gucci. The avenue also houses many fine bookstores, the most notable architecturally being Brentano's, housed in Ernest Flagg's outstanding structure of 1913 between 48th and 49th Streets. Other large bookstores include Doubleday, Dalton, Barnes & Noble and Rizzoli. In 1976 Skidmore, Owings & Merrill built the Olympic Tower on the corner of Fifth Avenue and 51st Street, marking a return of this part of the avenue to residential purposes. The photo was taken from a vantage point on the east side of the avenue between 48th and 49th Streets.

52. Sixth Avenue (Avenue of the Americas) *(opposite).* Sixth Avenue is one of the most varied streets in New York, and touches on many districts that are themselves of interest. Starting near the entrance to the Holland Tunnel at Canal Street, it runs uptown through Greenwich Village, where it passes 3rd, 4th and 8th Streets, all notable for their nightlife. During weekends especially, the sidewalks are usually packed with New Yorkers and tourists who wish to savor the activity of the Village. From 14th Street to 23rd Street the avenue runs through what was the city's fashionable department-store section between the 1870s and the First World War. Then covered by the Sixth Avenue el, these blocks bustled as customers flocked to stores such as B. Altman, Siegel-Cooper and Hugh O'Neill; many of these buildings, converted to other uses, still stand. Above 23rd Street are many discount stores specializing in electric appliances, as well as the wholesale flower district, centered around 27th Street; to see it at its busiest, the dedicated tourist should be there around dawn, when the city's florists are purchasing the day's supply of flowers. At 34th Street the avenue cuts across Herald Square, one of the city's most important shopping areas (see No. 40). Between 34th and 40th Streets the avenue forms the eastern boundary of the garment center, whose main artery is Seventh Avenue. In a welter of traffic one can see dresses destined for shops across the nation being pushed about on handtrucks, a primitive means of transportation that is just as firmly entrenched in the twentieth century as it was in the nineteenth. At 47th Street the avenue passes the diamond center, which runs across to Fifth Avenue. Here, under conditions of great security, are traded 80 percent of the diamonds sold in America. In the West 40s, the avenue begins to take on the radically different character shown here (this view has the east side of the block between 53rd and 54th in the foreground). In a futuristic vision, gleaming, monolithic office blocks rise from decorated public plazas. Until the early 1960s, most of the avenue at this level was lined with crumbling tenements that housed small businesses. The transformation that has taken place here is a striking example of how the city continually renews itself. The avenue ends at 59th Street (Central Park South) with its luxurious apartment houses and hotels. In 1945, as part of our Good Neighbor Policy, Sixth Avenue was renamed the Avenue of the Americas. But New Yorkers have never taken to the new name, and stubbornly continue to use the old one even though the city has spent a good deal of money mounting the seals of the American nations on the avenue's lampposts.

53. Rockefeller Center, between Fifth and Sixth Avenues at 50th Street *(above)*. To a large number of New Yorkers, including many architects, the finest and most important structures in the city are those that comprise Rockefeller Center. Although the complex rose in the 1930s, age has not detracted from the quality of its design and it remains unrivaled as one of the world's greatest examples of urban planning. The visionary project, the work of many architects (including Raymond Hood, Godley & Fouilhoux; Reinhard & Hofmeister; and Corbett, Harrison & MacMurray), rose between 1931 and 1940 on what had been Elgin's Botanical Garden a century before. The focus of the complex is the elegant, 70-story GE (formerly RCA) Building, faced with limestone and cast aluminum (as are the other buildings). In front of it, dramatically demonstrating how the planners designed the Center to accommodate all types of activity in a lively blend, is the famous skating rink, used as an outdoor restaurant in the summer. The promenade approach to the rink from Fifth Avenue is flanked with shops and little gardens whose plantings change with the seasons. Even at night, when the shops are closed and the offices fall silent, life continues at the Center as people attend Radio City Music Hall (No. 54) or dine and dance in the Rainbow Room atop the GE Building. The Center also has an amazing system of shops and restaurants arranged in underground concourses, in part inspired by those at Grand Central Station. The complex is also a living museum of Art Deco; major works include Paul Manship's statue of Prometheus (seen here), Lee Lawrie's statue of Atlas in front of the International Building, the murals in the main lobby of the GE Building by José María Sert and Frank Brangwyn and the spirited medallions on Radio City Music Hall by Hildreth Meière. Later works by such artists as Isamu Noguchi and Giacomo Manzù also decorate the Center.

54. Radio City Music Hall, Sixth Avenue and 50th Street *(opposite)*. Radio City is the last of the great movie palaces still in operation in New York City. It was opened in 1932, a flourishing period for the movies, which provided an escape from the problems of the Depression. Everything about the theater is on a colossal scale. The auditorium has a seating capacity of 6,200, making it the largest indoor theater in the world. The stage is also the world's largest, and the house boasts elaborate machinery—rain and steam curtains, turntables, stages and orchestra pit on hydraulic lifts, an enormous twin-console Wurlitzer organ—all of which may be called into play during one of the stage shows. The highlight of these extravagant presentations is the Rockettes, a corps of 36 precision dancers. Individually anonymous, the girls gain collective fame as they do their elaborate numbers. But the show at Radio City is not confined to the stage. The entire theater is one of the city's greatest showcases of Art Deco architecture and ornament. The grand foyer and other public lounges are beautifully preserved examples of the decoration of the period. In 1979 the theater abandoned its traditional presentation of movies paired with stage shows, and, after extensive restoration, reopened as a showcase for popular entertainers (while retaining its legendary Christmas and Easter spectaculars).

55. St. Patrick's Cathedral, Fifth Avenue between 50th and 51st Streets *(opposite).* St. Patrick's possesses one of the most imposing ecclesiastical facades in New York, as befits the Mother Church of the New York Archdiocese, the wealthiest in the country. In 1643 Father Isaac Jogues was the first Roman Catholic priest to visit New York, but the first congregation was not founded until 1785. In 1815 St. Patrick's Church was built as the cathedral church of the See of New York at Mott and Prince Streets. It still stands, but its appearance was greatly altered in 1868 after a fire. When New York was made an archdiocese in 1850, Archbishop John Hughes proposed that a new cathedral be built on the present site, then considered way "uptown," which had been in the church's possession since 1810. James Renwick, Jr., architect of Grace Church (No. 26), was selected to design the new cathedral. He began work on the plans in 1853, and in 1858 the cornerstone was laid. Although the cathedral was opened in 1879, the spires were not completed until 1888. The finished building, influenced by the cathedrals of Rheims and Cologne, is one of the foremost examples of the Gothic Revival. In 1906 the more delicate Lady Chapel, designed by Charles T. Matthews in the French Gothic Eclectic style, was added at the eastern end of the cathedral. The total exterior length of the building is 332 feet; the spires soar 330 feet above the street. The length of the interior is 307 feet, with a width of 124 feet. The transept, 96 feet wide, runs 144 feet. The ceiling vault rises 112 feet; suspended from it are the hats of the deceased Cardinal Archbishops of New York. The interior, with a seating capacity of about 2,500, is always filled on special occasions such as the Christmas and Easter services. Tickets are free, but must be secured well in advance.

The cathedral received a special honor on October 4, 1965, when Pope Paul VI visited it on the first papal journey to the United States.

56. St. Thomas' Church, Fifth Avenue and 53rd Street *(above).* In 1826 the Episcopal congregation of St. Thomas, having separated from Trinity Parish three years earlier, built its first church at Broadway and Houston Street. The structure, one of the earliest in the city in the Gothic manner, was destroyed by fire in 1851, but was rebuilt and reconsecrated the next year. When the nature of the neighborhood changed, the congregation decided to rebuild on the present location. The building was completed in 1870, but once again, in 1905, fire destroyed the congregation's church. The new structure, erected in 1914, was designed by Bertram Grosvenor Goodhue, one of the most important architects of Gothic buildings in New York. It is considered one of the city's finest churches, fusing elements of English and French Gothic and featuring an interplay of fine details with broad, plain surfaces. The massive corner tower is 214 feet long, 100 wide and 95 high. The interior of the church seats about 1,300 and is notable for its combination of grandeur with warmth through the liberal use of wood. The stained glass is fine, and the cross on the pillar to the right of the pulpit is made from stone that was taken from the Greek Chapel of the Church of the Holy Sepulchre in Jerusalem. The font contains medallions surviving from the old church. The south entrance is the Bride's Portal, through which have passed the brides of New York's most brilliant and wealthiest marriages. It is said that the intricate ornamentation above the door forms a dollar sign, which Goodhue wryly and secretly introduced.

57. Museum of Modern Art, 53rd Street between Fifth and Sixth Avenues *(above)*. The museum, one of the finest devoted to the modern visual arts, was founded in 1929 by Lillie P. Bliss, Mrs. Cornelius Sullivan and Abby Aldrich Rockefeller. Its original location was in the Hecksher Building at 57th Street and Fifth Avenue. The opening exhibition, *Cézanne, Gauguin, Seurat, Van Gogh,* had encouraging attendance (45,000 in the first month). The museum's popularity has increased manyfold, and it now attracts about a million visitors a year. The acquisition of its present site began in 1932. The building, by Philip L. Goodwin and Edward D. Stone, was dedicated by President Roosevelt in 1939. Since then it has undergone many extensions and alterations, including the addition of the charming Abby Aldrich Rockefeller Sculpture Garden, where concerts are given on many summer evenings. The museum has an invaluable library of books, and its Film Department possesses over 4,500 items. In 1939 it began showings of classic and unusual films. This program continues, attracting a faithful following of movie buffs and film scholars. Were it not for this collection, many of the films in it would have been lost. Among the many great paintings in the collection are works by Picasso, Monet, Rousseau and Modigliani. Among the sculptures are works by Calder, Rodin and Brancusi. Photography, an art form gaining in popularity, is represented by masters such as Steichen, Weston and Cartier-Bresson. Industrial exhibitions are one of the museum's specialties; the flags hanging outside the building in the photo advertise *Taxi*, an exhibit devoted to the most progressive designs for taxicabs.

58. Park Avenue *(opposite)*. Today Park Avenue is renowned for its luxury apartment houses and prestigious office buildings. In the nineteenth century it was scarred down its length by an open railway cut. Originally known as Fourth Avenue (a name that survives only below 14th Street), it was established as the right-of-way for the New York and Harlem Railroad in 1832. Grand Central Terminal was built on the avenue in 1871 (see No. 44) after the city had banned steam locomotives below 42nd Street because of the environmental blight. In 1902, when steam engines were banned from the city entirely, the New York Central was faced with a problem: it would either have to move its station to the city limits or convert to electricity. It chose the latter course. With the electrification of the line, it became possible to cover over the open cut. By the 1920s the avenue had developed a new character. It was lined by a few office buildings and hotels and many of the most sought-after luxury apartment buildings in the city. At that time the center malls running down the avenue were wider, allowing for more luxuriant plantings. In the 1950s the character of the avenue as far north as 59th Street began to change again. Many of the older buildings were demolished and new office towers of steel and glass rose in their place. In this photograph the transition from the glass-curtain office buildings to the older, stone-faced buildings above 59th Street is clearly noticeable. The elaborate cupola in the foreground belongs to the old New York Central Building, built by Warren & Wetmore in 1929; it formed a delightful termination to the vista down Park Avenue until the monolithic, overwhelming Pan Am Building (from which this photograph was taken) was constructed in 1963 (see No. 45).

59. Waldorf-Astoria, Park Avenue between 49th and 50th Streets *(opposite)*. The Waldorf-Astoria's reputation for luxury is so great that it has been called "America's unofficial palace." This location is the hotel's second. The original stood at Fifth Avenue and 34th Street, present site of the Empire State Building (No. 39); opened in 1893 as the Waldorf, it quickly became a favorite with New York's "Four Hundred." In 1897 a second hotel, the Astoria, was built adjacent to it. The two establishments were connected by a passageway that was called Peacock Alley from the dazzling parade of socialites who strutted back and forth from building to building in full finery. (In the present building the nickname is preserved as the name of a restaurant.) In 1928 the decision was made to move, and the new building, designed by Schultze & Weaver, was opened on October 1, 1931. The 47-story, 1,850-room, block-square hotel has maintained its position of favor with the rich and famous down to the present. Every President since Hoover has stayed there, as well as such heads of state as Queen Elizabeth II, the Shah of Iran, Emperor Hirohito, Golda Meir, Anwar El Sadat, Nikita Khrushchev and Prince Rainier III and Princess Grace of Monaco. The hotel has a collection of 125 national flags from which it can select the appropriate one to honor such dignitaries. The hotel has also housed such stars as Spencer Tracy, Maurice Chevalier, Melba Moore, Bing Crosby, Edith Piaf, Diana Ross, Merle Oberon, Carol Channing and Yul Brynner. The 28th to 42nd floors of the hotel contain suites, ranging from two to eight rooms, that are collectively called the Waldorf Towers; this area has a separate entrance on 50th Street and its own staff. Most of the suites are maintained as residences, though some are let by the day. Cole Porter was living at the Towers when he composed some of

his brightest songs, and the Duke and Duchess of Windsor maintained a suite as their New York residence. Even if a visitor cannot afford the luxury of the Waldorf, he should not miss the opportunity of walking through the lobby and public rooms to enjoy the hotel's many splendid examples of Art Deco.

60. St. Bartholomew's Church, Park Avenue between 50th and 51st Streets *(above)*. The history of this Episcopal congregation is associated with several buildings, each one built farther north than the last, reflecting the city's northward growth. The first divine services were held on January 11, 1835, at Military Hall, No. 193 The Bowery (then a fashionable neighborhood). A permanent site for the church was chosen at Great Jones Street and Lafayette Place; the new building was consecrated on October 12, 1836. But by 1871 the church was no longer adequate to the needs of the congregation and a new structure, built in the Lombardic style, was opened at Madison Avenue and 44th Street. In 1902 a new porch, designed by McKim, Mead and White after that of St. Giles's in Arles, France, was donated as a memorial to Cornelius Vanderbilt by his family. The first service at the present St. Bartholomew's was held on October 20, 1918. The building is a masterful interpretation of the Byzantine by Bertram Grosvenor Goodhue. With great skill he was able to incorporate the Vanderbilt porch from the previous 44th Street church into the new building without any jarring note. Inside the church are mosaics by Hildreth Meière — reminiscent of the famous works at Ravenna, Italy — that carry through the Byzantine theme. The Community House, on 50th Street, was dedicated in 1927 on the site of the old parish house, which had outlived its usefulness. It was the work of Mayers, Murray & Phillip.

61. Seagram Building, Park Avenue between 52nd and 53rd Streets *(opposite)*. Generally regarded as one of the finest examples of postwar architecture, the Seagram Building, built in 1958, started a trend in office buildings that still continues. The 38-story, bronze-dressed tower, set back on a handsome plaza with plantings and pools, was the result of the collaboration of the celebrated architects Mies van der Rohe, Philip Johnson and associate architects Kahn & Jacobs. Almost every feature, from the brown-tinted glass of the windows to the bathroom fixtures, was designed and made especially for the building. The Seagram Building is one of the few that have helped to enhance a corporate image through architectural achievement. Many buildings have followed the example of the Seagram, but few have come close to duplicating its cool elegance and loving attention to detail. In the foreground, looking much like a Florentine palazzo, is the Racquet and Tennis Club, one of the few relics in this area of Park Avenue's earlier days; the handsome

building, designed by McKim, Mead and White, was constructed in 1916–18.

62. Lever House, Park Avenue between 53rd and 54th Streets *(above)*. Lever House marked a revolutionary trend in New York office buildings. The work of Skidmore, Owings & Merrill, it was the first building in the city to use a slab tower with glass-curtain wall, giving the structure a lighter feeling than that projected by many skyscrapers constructed earlier. When Lever House was built in 1952, this section of lower Park Avenue was still primarily a residential bastion of wealthy New Yorkers. Its construction created a furor; while some appreciated its fine architectural principles, others lamented its lack of harmony with the staid mortar-and-brick apartment houses and hotels that lined the avenue. Today most of the apartments are gone, and the Lever House is less conspicuous among the office buildings that have followed its architectural inspiration. At the left is the Racquet and Tennis Club (see preceding caption).

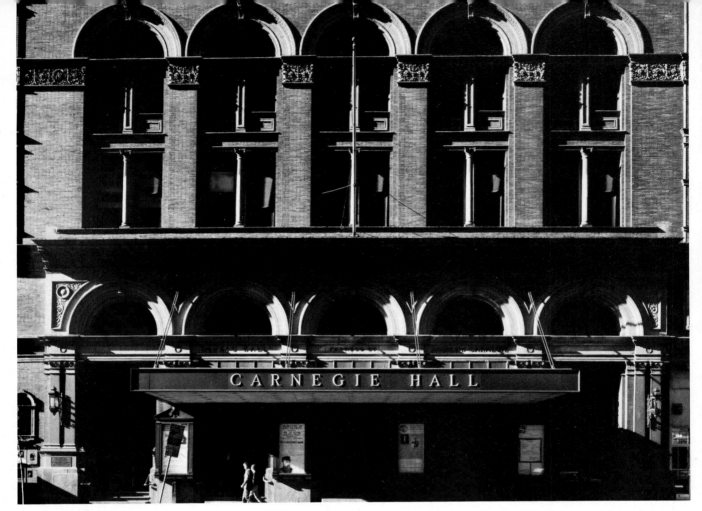

63. Carnegie Hall, 57th Street and Seventh Avenue *(above).*
Ever since its opening, Carnegie Hall has been famous as a
showcase for music of the highest international standards.
The wealthy philanthropist Andrew Carnegie undertook the
cost of construction after he was visited by Leopold
Damrosch, founder of the New York Symphony Society and
leader of the Oratorio Society, who explained that the ex-
isting concert halls in New York were inadequate. William B.
Tuttle designed the building in the Italian Renaissance style,
in consultation with Dankmar Adler and William Morris
Hunt. In 1891 a music festival was held to dedicate the hall,
during which Tchaikovsky conducted some of his own works.
The acoustics of the new hall were immediately acclaimed
and are held to be among the best in the world. In 1892 the
New York Philharmonic was formed, and played in Carnegie
Hall for 70 years. The impressive number of famous musicians who have performed in the 2,760-seat hall includes, to
name but a few: Mahler, Richard Strauss, Rachmaninoff,
Toscanini, Elman, Horowitz, Arthur Rubinstein, Dvořák
(who conducted the world premiere of his *New World Symphony* there), Josef Hofmann, Beecham, Solti, Von Karajan,
Paderewski and Benny Goodman. In 1962 the Philharmonic
moved to Philharmonic (now Avery Fisher) Hall in Lincoln
Center. For a while the future of Carnegie Hall was in doubt,
but a group headed by Isaac Stern saved it and it is now used
by many of the out-of-town orchestras whose visits help to
make New York's musical season one of the richest and most
diversified in the world. In 1986 renovations began on the hall,
vastly improving its appearance and comfort. Carnegie Hall
also houses a movie house and a recital hall, where many young
artists make their New York debuts. In the building are about
200 studios, cherished by people in the arts as ideal places for
practice, instruction and, occasionally, residence.

64. Plaza Hotel, Fifth Avenue and Central Park South *(opposite).* The Plaza Hotel is one of the last bastions of Edwardian
luxury in New York City. Designed by Henry J. Hardenbergh
in the French Renaissance Eclectic style, it was opened to the
public on October 1, 1907. This is the second Plaza Hotel to
stand on the site, the first having been opened in 1890. The
Plaza has always played host to the famous, among them Queen
Marie of Roumania, Frank Lloyd Wright, Enrico Caruso,
Eleanor Roosevelt, Brigitte Bardot, Lillian Russell and
Groucho Marx. Its most famous fictional habituée is Eloise,
the semibarbaric little girl created by Kay Thompson. The
hotel houses restaurants frequented by affluent New
Yorkers—the Oak Room, the Edwardian Room and the Palm
Court—as well as a ballroom which is the scene of many of the
city's glittering social and charity events. The hotel takes its
name from the Grand Army Plaza, one of New York's great
open spaces, which it fronts. Sculptor Karl Bitter had championed the planned and regulated development of the area since
1898, but the actual commission for the work on it went to
architect Thomas Hastings. Bitter's statue of Pomona stands on
top of the Pulitzer Fountain in the middle of the Plaza. The
night after he had completed the studio model of the statue,
Bitter was killed by an automobile as he and his wife left the old
Metropolitan Opera House. The statue was completed by one
of his assistants, and the whole fountain was finished in 1916.
Standing opposite the fountain is Augustus Saint-Gaudens'
William Tecumseh Sherman (1903), hailed as one of the major
equestrian statues of modern times. It depicts the general
being led by the figure of Victory. In front of the statue carriages can be hired for nostalgic, old-fashioned rides through
Central Park or down Fifth Avenue.

65. Columbus Circle, Central Park South and Central Park West *(opposite).* The intersection of Broadway, 59th Street (Central Park South) and Eighth Avenue at the southwest corner of Central Park creates Columbus Circle. Although the new Gulf & Western Building soars over the circle, the focus remains the proud statue of Columbus standing atop his pillar. The work of sculptor Gaetano Russo, it was unveiled in 1894, two years after the 400th anniversary of the great explorer's discovery of America. Opposite the Columbus statue, at the entrance to Central Park (just out of the picture at the right side), is the elaborate *Maine* Monument, a collaboration of architect H. Van Buren Magonigle and sculptor Attilio Piccirilli. Dedicated in 1913, the work commemorates the sinking of the battleship *Maine* in Havana Harbor, which sparked the Spanish-American War. A tablet affixed to the monument is supposed to be made from metal taken from the ship. To the south is the building that was originally erected to house Huntington Hartford's Gallery of Modern Art. This museum was short-lived, and the white-marble building, designed by Edward Durell Stone, has since been put to several uses. With so many unique buildings and works of sculpture, Columbus Circle should be one of the New York's great open spaces, but the area is unfortunately given over to endless vehicular traffic and fences.

66. Jacob K. Javits Convention Center of New York, Eleventh to Twelfth Avenues, 34th to 39th Streets *(above).* In 1986, years late because of construction and financial problems, the Javits Convention Center opened its 1.8-million-square-foot complex. Designed by I. M. Pei & Partners, it replaced the New York Coliseum in Columbus Circle as New York's principal exposition center. It houses shows that are open to the general public (boats, motorcycles, cars) as well as trade shows (computer graphics, pizza and fast food, contemporary furniture). The center's huge spaces (it can handle six major exhibitions simultaneously) are also used for banquets, graduations, press conferences and conventions. The center brings billions of dollars into New York, for visitors spend vast amounts on hotels, restaurants, transportation, shopping and entertainment, while the center itself generates nearly 90,000 jobs. This view shows the exterior of the 15-story Crystal Palace section, named after its precursor, Joseph Paxton's historic iron-and-glass structure built for London's Great Exhibition of 1851.

67. Central Park. An 840-acre island of green in a sea of concrete, Central Park represents an afterthought by the city fathers. When the grid plan of the city was laid out in 1811, no provision was made for a park; it was thought that New Yorkers seeking respite from the metropolis would simply take ferries to either the farmlands of Brooklyn or the wilds of New Jersey. In 1844 William Cullen Bryant called for the creation of a park in the city. The issue soon became political, and both candidates in the mayoral election of 1850 promised the creation of a park. The swampy land was purchased in 1856 for five and a half million dollars. The next year the commissioners declared an open competition for designs for the park. Frederick Law Olmsted, the great landscape architect and urban planner, in collaboration with Calvert Vaux, won with "Greensward," a plan that envisaged a series of wooded areas, open meadows, decorative waters, formal walks, sunken transverse carriage drives linking the east side of the city with the west (Olmsted and Vaux anticipated the urban growth around the park) and a drive encircling the park. To a substantial degree the original design of the park has been lost through the intrusion of various elements not intended by its creators: a zoo, a carousel, playing fields, skating rinks, a theater and restaurants. Nevertheless, as this view of boaters on the lake shows, people really enjoy the park. The bridge seen here was designed by Vaux, as were all of the park's original structures. In the distance rise the luxury apartment houses that line Central Park West. At the left are the twin towers of the Majestic (Irwin S. Chanin; 1930). In the center, distinguished by its triple-peaked roof, is Henry J. Hardenbergh's Dakota Apartments (1884); one of the city's first great apartment houses, it received its name because it was built so far from the developed section of the city that people said it might as well have been put up in the Dakota Territory. To the right of the Dakota is the Langham (Clinton & Russell; 1907). Above the foliage at the right are the two towers of the San Remo (Emery Roth; 1930).

68. Central Park Zoo, off Fifth Avenue at 64th Street *(above)*. In their original design for Central Park, Frederick Law Olmsted and Calvert Vaux made no provision for a zoological garden. New Yorkers, however, felt the need for one, and soon after the park was constructed a collection of pens and wooden buildings called the Menagerie was built in the park off Fifth Avenue at 64th Street. It contained a variety of animals donated by civic-minded New Yorkers, ranging from hippopotamuses and lions to rabbits and guinea pigs. In the 1930s, the zoo was remodeled in conjunction with the WPA, but by the 1970s it had become obvious that it was no longer consistent with the modern practice and philosophy of zoological gardens. Demolition of the buildings began in 1983, and on August 8, 1988, the new zoo was opened under the management of the New York Zoological Society. The zoo now features only species that can be properly taken care of in its 5.5 acres. It is divided into three ecological areas grouped around the Central Garden: the Tropical Zone, the Temperate Territory (shown here, in a view looking south) and the Polar Circle. The graceful design of the zoo buildings and landscape, created by Kevin Roche, John Dinkeloo & Associates, blends harmoniously with Central Park. Since the zoo attracts a remarkable cross section of New Yorkers of all classes and walks of life, the people-watching there is every bit as good as the animal-watching. Adjacent to the main zoo is the smaller Herbert Lehman Children's Zoo, where ducks, pigs, mice, sheep and other familiar animals are displayed in fanciful surroundings. The mortality rate among these specimens is high; they cannot resist the Cracker Jack, candied apples and other tasty but fatal bonbons the well-intentioned children offer them. The gateway leading from the main zoo to the children's zoo is topped by a wonderful musical clock that sports revolving animals. Adjacent to the zoo is the ivy-covered Arsenal. It was constructed from designs by Martin E. Thompson in 1847–48, years before the park was built. Today it houses the Parks Department, and the original plan for Central Park is displayed inside.

69. Metropolitan Opera House, Lincoln Center, Broadway at 63rd Street *(opposite)*. The Metropolitan Opera House is both the architectural focal point and the largest auditorium in Lincoln Center. The company has a long and distinguished history. The first Metropolitan Opera House, which stood on Broadway between 39th and 40th Streets, was opened in 1883 with a performance of *Faust*. Its interior was burnt out in 1892, but the auditorium was quickly rebuilt. Many of the world's legendary singers appeared there — Jean de Reszke, Nellie Melba, Enrico Caruso, Rosa Ponselle, Kirsten Flagstad, Lauritz Melchior, Lotte Lehmann and Maria Callas, to name a few. Toscanini conducted there, as did Mahler, Reiner, Walter and Solti. Beautiful as the old theater was, with its gold and red-plush interior, its sightlines were poor and the backstage facilities were antiquated. Proposals for a new house had been made since the 1920s, but only when the company threw its lot in with Lincoln Center did the long-desired move become a reality. Designed by Wallace K. Harrison, the new house was opened with a performance of an opera commissioned especially for the occasion, Samuel Barber's *Antony and Cleopatra*, with Leontyne Price as the doomed queen. The Metropolitan remains a "singer's house"; artists such as Nilsson, Sutherland and Pavarotti have all made regular appearances there. Although the new house may not have the charm of the old, it does have excellent acoustics, fine sightlines and ample room for intermission strolling. The auditorium and lobby are lighted by sparkling crystal chandeliers given by the Austrian Government. The interior walls are decorated with two Chagall murals (Chagall has also designed a production of *Die Zauberflöte* for the company). Once dominated by, and run primarily for, New York society, in recent years the Metropolitan Opera has made an effort to attract a wider audience. The opera season usually lasts from early fall through the spring. The house is sometimes used by visiting ballet troupes and opera companies during late spring and summer. Other principal structures at Lincoln Center include: Avery Fisher Hall, home of the New York Philharmonic; the New York State Theater, shared by the New York City Ballet and the New York City Opera; the New York Public Library for the Performing Arts; the Vivian Beaumont Theater; the Juilliard School of Music, one of the nation's foremost conservatories, which also contains Alice Tully Hall, an inviting wood-paneled auditorium, ideal for solo recitals and the performance of chamber music, where the New York Film Festival is held each fall.

70. New-York Historical Society, 77th Street and Central Park West *(opposite).* The New-York Historical Society houses not only one of the country's best collections of material pertaining to the city, but also one of the most impressive collections of Americana. Its holdings range from the charming bits of printed ephemera in the Landauer Collection to such important works of art as Audubon's *Birds of America*, Rembrandt Peale's portraits of George and Martha Washington and Thomas Cole's visionary series of paintings entitled *The Course of Empire*. Founded in 1804, the society was originally housed in City Hall. It moved several times, finally settling in the present structure, designed by York & Sawyer and built in 1903–08. It was enlarged by Walker & Gillette in 1938. By going through the museum's galleries, one can trace the development of New York City from earliest times down to the present. Highlights include fragments of the equestrian statue of George III that used to stand in Bowling Green and that was pulled down by inflamed patriots when the Declaration of Independence was first read in the city; old milestones; American silver and glass; carriages from the firm of Brewster and Company; furniture and toys. The library contains books, maps and documents that are priceless tools for research. *(Photograph by Victor Laredo)*

71. American Museum of Natural History, Central Park West between 77th and 81st Streets *(above).* Spread out over four floors, several wings, and almost 12 acres of exhibition space is one of the world's greatest scientific collections. Highlights of the exhibits include a vast collection of mammals, among them the habitat groups for which the museum is so famous; halls of birds, marine life, insects, reptiles, ethnology and geology. The banner over the entrance announces the new Hall of Minerals and Gems. The superb collection of fossil dinosaur skeletons includes a Tyrannosaurus Rex that towers 47 feet high and a Brontosaurus 67 feet long. In addition to its displays, the museum contains a library and sponsors scientific research. The museum's first building, on the 77th Street side, is basically a Victorian Gothic structure designed by Calvert Vaux and J. Wrey Mould and opened in 1877. Its present facade, however, as well as adjacent additions, are the work of J. C. Cady & Co.; dating from about 1890, this facade is considered one of the finest examples of Romanesque Revival architecture in the United States. The Theodore Roosevelt Memorial wing, fronting Central Park West, was designed by John Russell Pope in the Roman Eclectic style and completed in 1936. The equestrian statue of Roosevelt in front of it was executed by James Earle Fraser. Close observers will notice the resemblance of the Indian in the group to the one on the old Indian-head nickel — also the work of Fraser. Next to the museum is the Hayden Planetarium. In addition to its fascinating exhibits, the Planetarium offers unforgettable shows in its Sky Theatre, where a Zeiss projector can reproduce thousands of effects ranging from the aurora borealis to lunar and solar eclipses. The Laserium offers a more popular and spectacular exhibition, combining music with dazzling effects.

72. Upper East Side. The Upper East Side is the favored area of wealthy and fashionable New York. It is bounded roughly by 96th Street to the north, 59th Street to the south, Fifth Avenue to the west and the East River to the east. What it lacks in cohesiveness (it actually comprises several neighborhoods) it makes up for in the variety of its attractions. It also contains several ethnic enclaves, including Germans, Czechs and Hungarians. Residentially, it is divided into two main types of dwellings: the smart and architecturally distinguished town houses that line the side streets and the luxurious high rises (many of them co-ops) that have been built on the avenues. There is, however, some housing for the less affluent. Shopping on the East Side is aimed at the wealthy; many of the city's most exclusive shops are found on the avenues. Lexington Avenue boasts Bloomingdale's, perhaps the most popular department store with the affluent

and "trendy" middle class. Eating on the East Side runs the gamut from little snack shops that cater to famished shoppers grabbing a quick bite, to some of the most expensive restaurants in the country. Many middle-class New Yorkers prefer to play in the East Side too, for it contains many movie theaters, clubs and the much-publicized singles bars on First, Second and Third Avenues. The Upper East Side is also the art market of New York; many of the country's most important galleries and auction houses, such as Sotheby's, are on or near Madison Avenue. Pictured here is the residential intersection of 71st Street and Madison Avenue. On the northeast corner is the St. James' Episcopal Church, built in 1884 from designs by R. H. Robertson and rebuilt in 1924 by Ralph Adams Cram; it typifies the many brownstone churches that dotted the city during the last century.

73. Roosevelt Island, East River. One distinctive feature of the 1970s in New York was the development of large-scale housing projects along the waterfront. Independence Plaza was built along the Hudson; Waterside on the East River (see No. 35). By far the most ambitious and spectacular of these projects was the construction of the Roosevelt Island community, in the middle of the East River. The island on which it stands was purchased by the city in 1828 from the Blackwell family, which had owned it since the Colonial period, and whose name it bore. Because of its quietude, isolation and fresh air, some hospitals were built on it. With further expansion of other municipal facilities, it was renamed Welfare Island in 1921. In the late '60s it was proposed that the 2½-mile-long island now be used for residences. Sponsored by the New York Urban Development Corporation, Philip Johnson and John Burgee conceived a master plan for the community. Many of their plans were never adopted, others were substantially changed as the bankruptcy of the UDC forced various compromises to salvage the project. The island was given its present, more attractive, name in 1973.

By 1975 renting had begun. Housing varies from 20-story high rises to town houses, and accommodates lower-, middle- and upper-income families. Private vehicles are allowed only on Main Street; all other transportation is provided by minibuses. There are parks, baseball diamonds, shops and restaurants that furnish day-to-day services to the island's residents. Many of the older structures on the island have been incorporated into the new design. The old Blackwell farmhouse (1796) still stands, as do the old Smallpox Hospital (1856) and the central section of the Octagon Tower (1839) which had served as the New York City Lunatic Asylum. Cars can enter the island from the Roosevelt Island Bridge, which connects with Queens, and access by subway has been opened. Pedestrians, however, can travel over from Manhattan on the seven-million-dollar Swiss-designed tramway, seen here, which affords unforgettable views of the city. It is a striking engineering contribution to help solve problems of urban transportation with a public facility. Cars leave every few minutes during the rush hour, at longer intervals at other times.

74. Rockefeller University, York Avenue between 63rd and 68th Streets *(above)*. In 1901 John D. Rockefeller, Sr., founded the Rockefeller Institute for Medical Research. Known as The Rockefeller University since 1965, it has developed a high reputation for its outstanding work in the biomedical, behavioral and physical sciences. The program is devoted exclusively to research and graduate education leading to a PhD. Only about 20 of the most outstanding applicants are admitted to the program each year, and they study in a unique environment. The campus is small (only 15 acres) but so is the academic community — about 100 graduate fellows, 150 postgraduate investigators and 200 faculty members. There is a large supportive staff. The program avoids departmentalization and encourages students to cross over disciplines as their studies necessitate. The laboratory groups have made many solid contributions: the first demonstration of the properties of DNA in transmitting hereditary factors; the first continuous cultivation in a test tube of the parasite that causes malaria; important studies in cholesterol; the development of the methadone program of treating drug addiction. For such work alumni and faculty have won 16 Nobel prizes since 1912.

75. Temple Emanu-El, Fifth Avenue and 65th Street *(opposite)*. A Jewish community appeared in New Amsterdam only 20 years after it was founded. In 1654 a group of 23 Jews fled here from the Inquisition in Brazil. (The flagpole in Peter Minuit Plaza near Battery Park commemorates these settlers.) They formed Congregation Shearith Israel and built the first synagogue in the United States. Their first cemetery, at Chatham Square, is now a National Landmark. Those buried there include Benjamin Seixas, one of the founders of the New York Stock Exchange, and 18 soldiers who fought in the Revolution. Swollen by the waves of immigration at the turn of the century and by the refugees fleeing the Nazis, the city's Jewish population now numbers over two million, more than that in Tel Aviv. Temple Emanu-El houses one of the most distinguished congregations. Founded in 1845, it later combined with the congregation of Temple Beth-El. The nineteenth-century Temple Emanu-El, in Moorish style, stood at Fifth Avenue and 43rd Street, and was the work of the distinguished architect Leopold Eidlitz. The present temple, the largest Reform synagogue in the United States, was completed in September 1929. Its architects were Robert D. Kohn, Charles Butler and Clarence S. Stein. The auditorium, with its rich ornamentation, roughly follows the basilica plan found in early Italian churches. It can accommodate about 2,500 worshippers. The Temple also contains a chapel (Byzantine in style), the Isaac M. Wise Memorial Hall seating 1,500, a Community House and a Religious School. The Temple's extensive collection of Judaica is an important tool to scholars. Temple Emanu-El's Friday-night services are broadcast locally over radio station WQXR.

76. Frick Collection, Fifth Avenue and 70th Street (above). Henry Clay Frick was a man with two sides to his nature. As an associate of Andrew Carnegie in the steel industry, he was noted for his ruthless tactics. It was Frick who called out the Pinkertons during the notorious Homestead strike in 1892. (He himself was shot and stabbed during the strike.) As a devoted collector of art his tastes were wide and refined. His palatial residence on Fifth Avenue, designed in the Louis XVI style by Carrère & Hastings, was completed in 1914. It stands on the site of the old Lenox Library, the holdings of which had been transferred to the New York Public Library (No. 43). Frick did not enjoy his mansion for long; he died in 1919. His wife lived there until her death in 1931. Then, according to stipulations in Frick's will, the building underwent alterations to allow it to be opened to the public as an art gallery. The central carriage drive was roofed over with glass, and a delightful pool with bronze frogs spouting water was installed. An art reference library was constructed behind the house. The work was designed and supervised by John Russell Pope. The building was opened in 1935. With the collection bequeathed by Frick as a basis, the trustees have added important works over the years. The rooms open to the public on the ground floor, however, retain much of the character they had while Frick lived in the mansion. Since the paintings are arranged purely visually, and not according to period or school, there is an unacademic vitality to the display. The rooms are packed with priceless works: Titians, Rembrandts, El Grecos, Holbeins, Turners, Whistlers, magnificent period furniture and rare books. Especially delightful is the Boucher Room containing paintings designed for Mme. de Pompadour. The Fragonard Room (originally Mrs. Frick's boudoir) contains the painted cycle *The Progress of Love*, commissioned by Mme. du Barry. (The Fragonards, as well as other works, were acquired from Joseph Duveen,

one of the most influential and colorful art dealers of the period.) In 1976 a new entrance and foyer were added to the building on 70th Street.

77. Whitney Museum of American Art, Madison Avenue and 75th Street (opposite). The striking granite-faced building is the third home of the museum, which had its origin in the Whitney Studio Club, founded by Gertrude Vanderbilt Whitney in 1918. A sculptor herself (among her works are the statue of Stuyvesant in Stuyvesant Square and the Washington Heights War Memorial at 168th Street and Broadway), Mrs. Whitney felt that American artists, whether avant-garde or conservative, deserved encouragement and adequate public exposure. The Club disbanded in 1928, and in 1931 Mrs. Whitney opened the Whitney Museum of American Art on West 8th Street. She died in 1942, but members of the family continue to take an active part in the museum's affairs. Carrying on an active program of acquisitions that soon necessitated larger quarters, the museum moved to West 54th Street, next to The Museum of Modern Art, in 1954. Again space proved too confined, and in 1966 the museum moved to its present quarters, designed by Marcel Breuer. In 1986, still plagued by problems of space, the museum announced controversial plans for further expansion. The museum's policies continue those of Mrs. Whitney. Its collection consists entirely of American paintings, prints, drawings and sculpture. Photography, architecture and design are outside its scope. The museum feels that it has a special commitment to talented living artists; its annual exhibition of new works is one of the highlights of the art season. There are no judges or jury, and no prizes are given. The museum also mounts from three to seven special exhibitions a year. In the photo, a large model of Hiram Powers' *Greek Slave* announces a Bicentennial exhibition of American sculpture.

78. Metropolitan Museum of Art, Fifth Avenue between 80th and 84th Streets. The Metropolitan Museum of Art ranks with such institutions as the Louvre, the British Museum and the Prado as one of the world's greatest museums. The imposing central section on Fifth Avenue at 82nd Street was erected in 1894–1902 (Richard Morris Hunt, principal architect); other portions date from as early as 1880. Through the years the building has had many alterations and additions, sometimes over the objections of those New Yorkers who feel that the structure is encroaching too far into Central Park. When the Lehman Wing was opened, its design was the center of heated debate. Another incursion into the park was made for the installation of the Temple of Dendur, brought to this country block by block from its original site in Egypt. Strangely, the piles of masonry over the entablatures of the facade, originally intended to be sculptured, remain uncut. The interior of the building, especially the huge entrance hall reminiscent of Roman baths, is equally impressive. The size and scope of the collections contained within the building are almost beyond belief. Among the many separate collections are: European paintings (featuring works by the great masters such as Rembrandt, Goya, Titian and Monet); American painting and sculpture from the Primitives and the Hudson River School to Jackson Pollock; a brilliant assemblage of arms and armor; the Costume Institute, which stages some of the most glamorous exhibitions in the city; Egyptian art; Islamic Art; a Greek and Roman collection; European decorative arts. A junior museum and extensive educational program add further to the museum's resources. Local colleges and universities rely on it to enrich their courses.

79. Solomon R. Guggenheim Museum, Fifth Avenue between 88th and 89th Streets. The Guggenheim is a distinguished collection housed in an equally distinguished building. Solomon Guggenheim, a member of one of New York's wealthiest families, acquired a taste for modern art in the 1920s, when he met Delaunay, Kandinsky, Chagall and other painters. At a time when most millionaires were still seeking Old Masters, Guggenheim began acquiring modern works on a large scale. Soon he had to rent studio space for his collection. In 1937 the collection was incorporated into a foundation. Two years later the museum opened on East 54th Street, the first of several temporary locations. In 1943 Guggenheim engaged Frank Lloyd Wright to design a permanent building; by 1951 all the necessary land had been purchased. Guggenheim died in 1949, but he had seen all the plans, and work continued. Actual construction of the museum, the only Wright public building in New York City, lasted from 1957 to 1959. The structure was the center of tremendous controversy. Conservative New Yorkers claimed that the "giant snail" was a blight on prestigious Fifth Avenue. Others championed it as the work of one of America's most gifted and influential architects. The controversy is over now; the building is accepted as a valuable part of New York's architectural fabric. The interior of the museum consists of a coiled ramp stretching over a quarter of a mile at a three-percent grade. The 74 bays in which the paintings are displayed are illuminated principally by natural light. The dome rises 92 feet above the main floor. In addition, the museum has an auditorium seating 299 people, a restaurant and a bookstore, as well as storage and administrative space. Several additions have been made to the building, and late in 1990 the entire museum was temporarily closed so that a major addition (the subject of heated controversy) could be erected.

80. Gracie Mansion, Carl Schurz Park, East End Avenue at 89th Street. One of the most beautiful residences in the city, and one of the best examples of Federal architecture, Gracie Mansion stands amid the greenery of Carl Schurz Park, with a fine view of the Hell Gate stretch of the East River. The house was erected by Archibald Gracie, a prosperous merchant, in 1799, when everything north of Canal Street was farmland or estates. Famous visitors in its early years included Alexander Hamilton, DeWitt Clinton, Lafayette, Washington Irving, Louis-Philippe and John Quincy Adams. The city purchased the house and property in 1887. In 1923 the Museum of the City of New York (see No. 81) was established and occupied the mansion until its present premises on Fifth Avenue were completed in the early 1930s. In 1942 the city began using the mansion as a residence for its mayors. Fiorello La Guardia, one of the city's most flamboy-

ant and best-loved mayors, was the first to inhabit it. In 1966 an annex was built; designed by Mott B. Schmidt and named the Susan B. Wagner Wing, in honor of the late wife of former mayor Robert Wagner, it provides public spaces in which the mayor can entertain guests and visiting dignitaries. The new addition blends harmoniously with the old building. The park in which the house stands is named after one of the most influential of the nineteenth-century German immigrants to this country. Fleeing his homeland after the Revolution of 1848, Schurz quickly adapted to life in this country, becoming a Union major-general in the Civil War, a Senator, Secretary of the Interior and a leading figure in the press. He was living in the Yorkville neighborhood, not far from the park, when he died in 1906. The area long maintained a German atmosphere.

81. Museum of the City of New York, Fifth Avenue between 103rd and 104th Streets. Founded in 1923 and housed in Gracie Mansion, in 1932 the museum moved to its present five-story building of red brick and marble, designed by Joseph H. Freedlander. The museum is devoted entirely to the history of the city, and has exhibits on every stage of New York's history and development, beginning with the Dutch and English Gallery on the first floor and culminating in the John D. Rockefeller Rooms (taken intact from their original site at 4 West 54th Street) on the fifth floor. Highlights of the museum include lifelike dioramas reconstructing the past,

the toy gallery, a fine collection of silver, and the Duncan Phyfe drawing room. Of particular value to scholars are the Theatre & Music Collection and the superb assemblage of photographs of the city, prominent among which are those taken by the Byron brothers and Jacob Riis at the turn of the century — an invaluable documentation of old New York. Children delight in the "Please Touch" exhibition, in which they are invited to handle antique objects. The museum expands its activities to encompass the whole city. It is noted for its architectural and historical walking tours through various neighborhoods of New York.

82. Cathedral of St. John the Divine, Amsterdam Avenue and 112th Street. If it had been completed as planned, the Cathedral of St. John the Divine would be the largest in the world; but in its present state, it is known by many New Yorkers as "St. John's the Unfinished." Nevertheless, Americans are an impatient breed; many of the most beautiful cathedrals in Europe took centuries to be completed. The building was begun in 1892, following Romanesque Eclectic plans by Heins & La Farge that had been selected in open competition. In 1911, when the apse, crossing and choir had been constructed, supervision of the work passed on to Ralph Adams Cram of Cram & Ferguson, who decided to continue in the French Gothic Eclectic style. Work had been completed on the new crossing, nave and transept by the Second World War, when building ceased. The interior is extremely impressive; the nave is more than 600 feet long and its arches soar 124 feet. Concerts and dramatic events are occasionally held in the Cathedral, its majestic spaces compensating for its echoing acoustics. In 1978 it was announced that the two towers would be completed according to a modified plan. Local residents were trained in the ancient art of stonemasonry and work was resumed.

83. Columbia University, Broadway and 116th Street *(left, above)*. Columbia's history is closely tied to that of New York City and the nation. The college (the men's undergraduate division of the university) was originally created as King's College under a royal charter in 1754. The first class met in the vestryroom of Trinity Church (see No. 11). In 1760 the school moved to new premises in the Chelsea area near the Hudson River. The president of the college at the time of the Revolution was Rev. Myles Cooper. He was attacked by a mob in 1775 and managed to escape to England. Patriots who were educated at the college included Alexander Hamilton, John Jay and Gouverneur Morris. At the end of the war the college was given its present name, more in keeping with the nature of the new republic. In the middle of the nineteenth century the school, by then a university, moved to new quarters bounded by Madison and Lexington Avenues and 49th and 50th Streets. The university grew rapidly. In the 1890s it moved to its present location. (A small building that stands just to the right outside of the view in this photograph is the last survivor of the Bloomingdale Insane Asylum, which stood on the site before the university purchased it.) The general plan of the new grounds, as well as most of the original buildings, were the work of McKim, Mead and White. Featured in this photo is Low Library, built 1893–97. Approached by a broad, imposing flight of stairs, it is one of the firm's best designs. The shallow dome was inspired by that of the Pantheon in Rome. The Roman Eclectic building makes an interesting foil to the Neo-Gothic tower of Riverside Church, seen just to the left of it. Low Library now serves as the administrative center of the university. The bulk of the actual library is now in Butler Library, on the South Campus. On the steps in front of Low Library is Daniel Chester French's sculpture *Alma Mater* (1903).

84. Grant's Tomb, Riverside Drive and 122nd Street *(left, below)*. After his brilliant success as Supreme Commander of the Union forces in the Civil War, Ulysses Simpson Grant was elected President in 1868 and was reelected in 1872. His administration, however, was clouded by scandal. In his final years he traveled and lost money in unsuccessful business ventures. Learning that he had terminal cancer, he tried to provide for his family by writing and selling his memoirs. On July 23, 1885, he died. It was decided that he would be buried in New York, and he was interred in a temporary vault, not far from the site of the present tomb. Money for the construction of a permanent structure was contributed by 90,000 citizens and the monument was dedicated on April 27, 1897. John H. Duncan designed the memorial (based on reconstructions of the fragmentary Mausoleum at Halicarnassus) using a variety of classic orders: fluted Doric columns in the portico, Ionic columns supporting the rotunda. The sculptural decoration is by John Massey Rhind. Grant's sarcophagus lies in the open crypt under the rotunda; that containing the remains of Julia Grant was placed next to it in 1902. The interior also contains mementos of Grant's life: murals mapping out his major Civil War battles; mosaics of Vicksburg, Chattanooga and the surrender at Appomattox; regimental flags; and busts of the Union officers McPherson, Ord, Thomas, Sherman and Sheridan. The monument became the Grant National Memorial in 1958; its administration was given to the National Park Service the next year. In 1972, in recognition of Grant's achievement in helping to create Yellowstone, America's first national park, the Grant Centennial Plaza was erected around the monument. Supervised principally by the local community, it consists of freeform benches gaily decorated with colorful mosaics, and is especially popular with the neighborhood children. Its presence somewhat softens and humanizes the grim and imposing tomb.

85. Riverside Church, Riverside Drive between 120th and 122nd Streets. Most prominent among the institutional structures of the Upper West Side is the soaring tower of Riverside Church. Richly designed by Allen & Collens and Henry C. Pelton, the building, opened in 1930, was one of the last of the grand ecclesiastical structures erected in New York. The costs were borne by John D. Rockefeller, Jr. The 21-story, 392-foot tower houses offices, including the studios of radio station WRVR. The top of the tower has an observation plat-form that commands a fine view, and houses the Laura Spelman Rockefeller Memorial Carillon, the world's largest with its 74 bells. The church is extremely active, containing such facilities as a community center and theater, classrooms, a nursery, a library and a cafeteria. Among its many works of art are a late fifteenth-century Flemish tapestry and *Madonna and Child*, a splendid modern sculpture by Sir Jacob Epstein.

86. Hispanic Society of America, Audubon Terrace, Broadway and 155th Street. In 1904 millionaire Archer Huntington, who had been eagerly collecting Spanish artworks since his first visit to Spain in 1892, established the Hispanic Society to further the appreciation of the Iberian cultures in the United States. In 1908 the present building, designed by Charles Pratt Huntington, a cousin of Archer Huntington, was opened. It was enlarged between 1910 and 1926. The museum is approached through an impressive courtyard; the entire complex, known as Audubon Terrace, houses several distinguished institutions of learning. The central statue (here seen through the gateway) depicts El Cid. This work, as well as the animal sculptures and the bas-reliefs of Boabdil and Don Quixote, was the work of Anna Vaughn Hyatt Huntington, the wife of the founder and one of America's leading academic sculptors. Housed in the museum are many of the finest examples of Spanish and Portuguese art and culture to be found outside the Iberian peninsula. Perhaps the most famous item is Goya's enigmatic portrait of the Duchess of Alba, one of his finest works. Other Goyas in the collection include his stunning etchings of bullfights. Paintings by masters such as Velázquez and El Greco are also on view. The library has over 100,000 books, hundreds of them incunabula. The collection also features textiles, pottery and tiles, silver and gold and choice items from colonial Spanish America.

87. Striver's Row (St. Nicholas Historic District), 138th to 139th Street, between Seventh and Eighth Avenues. The elegant town houses of Striver's Row seem far removed from Harlem, in which they stand, and affirm the fact that, although Harlem may be a ghetto plagued with the problems that afflict many inner-city communities throughout the nation, it is diverse and has much to offer. The village of Nieuw Haarlem was founded by Peter Stuyvesant in 1658 in an area that had been settled since 1637. Its rustic qualities began to disappear in 1837, when the opening of railroad ties made access from the city downtown easy, spurring development as an affluent suburb. As more lines and the subway (1904) were added, a building boom changed the face of Harlem, distinguished by some of the most attractive housing in New York. But the realtors' unbounded optimism led to overdevelopment, and many houses remained unsold and apartments unrented at just the time when the housing in the traditional black section of New York, in the lower West 30s, was being demolished to make way for such projects as Pennsylvania Station and Macy's. A black developer, Philip A. Payton, Jr., saw his opporunity, and was soon selling Harlem housing to blacks. Harlem re-

tained a white population through the 1920s, when the black presence grew, and eventually predominated. Harlem flourished as a center for black culture, enjoying its heyday during the 1920s, when its nightlife attained international fame. (Many of its most famous clubs were, in fact, closed to blacks.) Although Harlem was hard-hit by the Depression and never recovered its earlier luster, over the years the number of influential blacks who have either lived in, or been inspired by, Harlem has been considerable, from W. E. B. Du Bois, Marcus Garvey, Langston Hughes and Paul Laurence Dunbar to Richard Wright, James Baldwin, Malcolm X and LeRoi Jones. Striver's Row, in fact, took its name from a 1933 play by Abram Hill, who had founded the American Negro Theater. The houses had been built for David H. King in 1891, the various rows being designed by some of the leading architects of the day: James Brown Lord (whose neo-Georgian facades are seen here); Bruce Price and Clarence S. Luce; and McKim, Mead and White. By 1919, the white families that had lived in them were moving out, their places being taken by successful blacks. Residents have included W. C. Handy and Eubie Blake.

88. George Washington Bridge, 179th Street (Hudson River) *(opposite)*. The possibility of constructing a bridge across the Hudson to link New York with New Jersey was first discussed early in the nineteenth century. In 1868, a year before construction began on the Brooklyn Bridge, the Hudson River Bridge Company was granted a charter, but the enterprise came to nothing. By the beginning of this century, however, the need for a bridge had become more pressing because of the increased traffic between the two states and the inadequacy of the ferry service. In 1925 the Port Authority was given approval to construct the bridge. It was designed by the Authority under the supervision of O. H. Ammann, with Cass Gilbert as consulting architect. Ground was broken on September 21, 1927 and the bridge was dedicated on October 24, 1931—almost a year ahead of schedule. With a span of 3,500 feet, it was at the time the longest suspension bridge in the country. (The 4,200-foot Golden Gate Bridge in San Francisco was opened in 1937; the distinction now belongs to the Verrazano-Narrows Bridge; see No. 99.) Over 107,000 miles of wire were spun into the cables of the George Washington Bridge by John A. Roebling's Sons Company. The two towers, each soaring 635 feet above the water, were originally intended to be clad with concrete and granite; but the public and builders were so pleased with their appearance that they were left bare. Although the bridge lost some of its feeling of airy lightness when a second deck was added in 1962 to handle increased traffic, it remains one of the most beautiful in the world. In the background are the high-rise apartments of Fort Lee, New Jersey, atop the Palisades.

89. Cloisters, Fort Tryon Park, Broadway north of 193rd Street *(above)*. At the Cloisters a bit of medieval Europe flourishes in New York. Built in 1934–38 with funds provided by John D. Rockefeller, Jr., the structure houses part of the medieval collection of the Metropolitan Museum of Art (see No. 78). The setting itself is magnificent, atop a hill in the middle of Fort Tryon Park, with breathtaking views of the Hudson and the Palisades. One of the pleasures of visiting the Cloisters frequently is to view the seasonal changes in scenery. Several medieval European cloisters have been reassembled in the museum, giving it its name. The reassembly, as well as the total museum design, was carried out by Charles Collens of Allen, Collens & Willis. The reconstruction was done conscientiously; diagrams on the cloister walls indicate which elements are original and which are modern replacements. (These replacement parts were made from stone taken from the quarries in southern France that were used when the buildings were first constructed.) The gardens enclosed by the cloisters are delightful, and exude a sense of peace and serenity. Also included in the museum are the twelfth-century Fuentidueña Chapel and other medieval chapels. Bibliophiles will delight in the *Très Riches Heures* of Jean, Duc de Berry, one of the world's great illuminated books. Perhaps the most famous pieces at the Cloisters are the Unicorn Tapestries, an early sixteenth-century series depicting the capture of the fabled beast. The collection also contains many liturgical items such as the celebrated Chalice of Antioch. Surrounded by exquisite painting, sculpture, carvings and architecture, looking out onto a sun-dappled garden and listening to one of the frequent concerts of medieval music, the visitor sometimes has difficulty remembering that the Cloisters stands in one of the world's youngest and busiest cities.

90. Yankee Stadium, River Avenue and 157th Street, Bronx
(above). Few structures in New York have echoed with as
many cheers — and occasional groans of disappointment —
as has Yankee Stadium. For New Yorkers love baseball pas-
sionately and are especially proud of their Yankees. On April
18, 1923, the first game was played in the stadium, when the
Yankees defeated the Boston Red Sox 4–1. Appropriately
enough, the immortal Babe Ruth hit the first home run in the
stadium during that game. (In fact, the stadium has been
called "The House That Ruth Built.") Prior to its construction, the Yankees had played at the Polo Grounds. In the
years since, many greats have thrilled the crowds: Ruth, Lou
Gehrig, Joe DiMaggio, Mickey Mantle and Reggie Jackson.
Between 1974 and 1976 the stadium underwent a complete
renovation. When it was completed, the seating capacity was
57,545, making it the sixth-largest stadium in the
Hemisphere. The stadium has been used for events other than
baseball. The Giants football team played there between
1956 and 1972, when it left New York. Jehovah's Witnesses
have held their meetings there and, on October 4, 1965,
visiting Pope Paul VI held a mass in the vast space at which
80,000 worshippers attended. New York is fortunate in having another baseball stadium, Shea Stadium in Queens, home
of the New York Mets. (*Photo courtesy of The New York
Yankees*)

91. New York Botanical Garden, Bronx Park *(opposite, top)*.
Inspired by the example of London's famous Kew Gardens,
the New York Botanical Garden was founded in 1891. The
design was the work of Calvert Vaux, who years earlier had
collaborated with Frederick Law Olmsted on Central Park,
and Samuel Parsons, Jr., after whom Parsons Boulevard in
Queens is named. The 230-acre garden has become one of the
most important in the world. The delightful grounds feature
over 12,000 species of plants of all descriptions. Lord & Burnham's great conservatory of cast iron and glass was influenced by Paxton's Crystal Palace of 1851 in London. In 1978

it was renamed the Enid A. Haupt Conservatory in honor of
the benefactress who sponsored the restoration it desperately
needed. The visitor can walk through the building, enjoying
its exotic tropical plants. Another of the garden's major structures, the Museum Building, is seen in the photograph. Designed by Robert W. Gibson in the Beaux-Arts style and completed in 1902, it contains a shop that sells plants, a library of
70,000 volumes and many periodicals, and a unique her-
barium (open to scholars only) with over three million dried
specimens. The garden is also remarkable for preserving a
large section of the Bronx River Gorge, which runs through
the grounds, as well as an indigenous hemlock forest. A
restaurant operates in the old Lorillard Snuff Mill (ca. 1840);
in season, visitors can eat out on the terrace with a fine view
of the Bronx River.

92. New York Zoological Park (Bronx Zoo), Bronx Park *(opposite, bottom)*. The Bronx Zoo, the largest in the nation, was
opened in 1899. It was one of the first to eliminate the small,
claustrophobic cages that were once the only type of animal
housing in American and European zoos. Most of the Bronx
Zoo's 252 acres are divided into several environments where
animals roam free, in approximations of their surroundings
in the wild. Some traces of the older system do, however, remain, such as the Elephant House, shown here; the work of
the original architects, Heins & La Farge, it was opened in
1911. The zoo has many unforgettable exhibits, including the
World of Darkness (which features nocturnal animals), the
World of Birds (an outstanding aviary in which a tropical
rainstorm occurs every day at two o'clock), an African environment with lions, gazelles, antelope and zebra, a South
American group and the ever-popular monkey house. Wild
Asia is an environment viewed by the public from cars on a
monorail. Its 38 acres contain a tahr herd, tigers, rhinos and
elephants. Institutions such as the Bronx Zoo have gained
additional importance as the last refuge for many species that
are faced with extinction in the wild.

93. Brooklyn Heights, Brooklyn. Bounded roughly by the Brooklyn-Queens Expressway to the north, the Esplanade to the west, Atlantic Avenue to the south and Henry, Clinton and Court Streets to the east, Brooklyn Heights claims the distinction of being New York's first suburb. In 1814 Robert Fulton's ferry *Nassau* began operation on the route between the Heights and Manhattan. Bankers and merchants in lower Manhattan quickly realized that with the new ferry service the Heights was highly desirable as a residential neighborhood. It was quickly developed and flourished through the end of the century. The comparative isolation that had appealed to the upper- and middle-class population of the Heights was lessened by the opening of the Brooklyn Bridge in 1883 and by that of the subways in 1908. Much of the area deteriorated until the middle of this century, when its charms were rediscovered. In 1965 the Heights was declared New York's first Landmark District, affording it considerable protection. Today it is possible to walk through its tree-lined streets and enjoy the great variety of domestic architecture built before 1860. The Heights has many strong historic links. Henry Ward Beecher, brother of Harriet Beecher Stowe, preached passionate abolitionist sermons from the pulpit of the Plymouth Church on Orange Street. Shortly before the Civil War he electrified the city by auctioning off a slave in the church to drive home the horror of slavery; the money raised was used to buy the girl's freedom. Abraham Lincoln worshipped in pew 89 of the same church, and speakers there have included Charles Dickens, Mark Twain, William Lloyd Garrison, John Greenleaf Whittier and Booker T. Washington. Nearby, in a now demolished store on Fulton Street, Walt Whitman had the first edition of *Leaves of Grass* printed. The Nobel prize-winning Norwegian novelist Sigrid Undset lived at the Hotel Margaret and Thomas Wolfe wrote *Of Time and the River* while living at No. 5 Montague Terrace. As the Heights has enjoyed its renaissance, many new and charming shops have opened on Montague Street and along Atlantic Avenue, where there is a large Arab community. The Esplanade, seen in the photograph, offers a spectacular view of the New York skyline. Rising highest are the twin towers of the World Trade Center (No. 13); slightly left of center is the Woolworth Building (No. 15); at the right is Brooklyn Bridge (No. 16).

94. Brooklyn Museum, Eastern Parkway at Washington Avenue, Brooklyn *(above, left)*. The Brooklyn Museum is one of the foremost museums in the country, famous for its collection of ancient Egyptian and Coptic antiquities, which is considered by many scholars to be the finest in the Western Hemisphere. The museum's collection of American paintings is also highly regarded, as are its displays of primitive and pre-Columbian art. Other attractions include a fine group of period rooms, including the entire Schenck House, dating from 1675, which originally stood in the Flatlands section of Brooklyn. Hals, Cranach the Elder, Matisse, Cézanne and Degas are among the masters represented in the collection of European paintings. Behind the museum is the unusual Frieda Schiff Warburg Sculpture Garden. Opened in 1966, its art works come from the facades of New York City buildings that have been demolished. The museum itself is housed in an imposing building erected in 1897 from designs by McKim, Mead and White in the Neoclassic style. The building as it stands represents but a fraction of the original design, which was never completed. In 1936 the massive steps that led to the portico were removed, somewhat spoiling the appearance of the building. The main lobby, in a severe Art Deco style, is entered directly from the street.

95. Brooklyn Botanic Garden, between Washington and Flatbush Avenues, Brooklyn *(above, right)*. Although it is spread over only 50 acres, as compared to the New York Botanical Garden's 230 (see No. 91), the Brooklyn Botanic Garden contains a tremendous variety of plants in many different settings. It is perhaps most famous for its Japanese gardens and plantings. Every spring thousands flock to see its Japanese cherry trees in bloom. In 1915 Takeo Shiota's stroll garden (seen here), based on those of the Momoyama period, was opened. Here a visitor can pause in a teahouse (where no tea is to be had) and look at the *torii* set in the little lake, backed by a waterfall and plantings. A reproduction of Kyoto's Ryoanji Temple Garden was opened in 1963. The Brooklyn Botanic Garden also has one of the finest collections of bonsai — Japanese miniature trees — in this part of the world. Other features include a scent garden for the blind, formal rose and iris gardens, shady paths, and a meadow crossed by a stream where Brooklyn children delight in catching tadpoles in the spring. The greenhouses are worthy of note, especially those devoted to primitive forms of vegetation such as the cycads. The Palladian-style Administration Building, built in 1918 from plans by McKim, Mead and White, adds a dignified note.

96. Prospect Park, Brooklyn *(opposite)*. One of the world's great places for public recreation, Prospect Park is the result of the collaboration of Frederick Law Olmsted and Calvert Vaux, the men who had designed Central Park. The idea of developing the park was first conceived in 1859. Brooklyn was then a separate city in rivalry with New York and wanted to have a park that would outshine Central Park, which was then being landscaped. The Civil War, however, delayed work on Prospect Park. In 1865 Vaux and the great Brooklyn civic leader James T. Stranahan decided that an earlier plan submitted was unsatisfactory, and altered the boundaries of the proposed park. (Ironically, Prospect Hill, from which the park takes its name, was left outside the 526-acre park by this change.) When the boundaries of the park were established, Vaux encouraged Olmsted, who was in California, to come to Brooklyn to work on the landscaping. The result has been held by many, including Olmsted and Vaux themselves, to be superior to Central Park. Prospect Park embodies all the best features of Central Park with refinements and improvements based on the architects' experience. The masterly landscaping includes waters, woodlands, and open lawns, all of which offer constantly changing views that disguise the fact that the park is in the middle of a great city. Since Brooklyn's skyline is lower than Manhattan's, it intrudes less on the rustic mood the two men created. There have also been fewer encroachments, although the park does have a zoo, carousel and other amenities. The photograph shows the boathouse, designed by Helmle & Huberty after a Venetian building and erected on the Lullwater in 1904. Its fine terra-cotta facade had deteriorated badly, but was lovingly restored in 1973, and the boathouse is now one of the showplaces of the park.

97. Coney Island, Brooklyn. An off-season view shows the "playground of millions" with only a handful of people on its six-mile beach. On a summer day, however, the beach can be packed with over a million people, all battling for a few feet of space. It was Coney Island's surf and cooling breezes that originally made it a resort for the upper classes in the middle of the last century and the site of large, elegant hotels. Toward the end of the century, however, improved transportation made access easier for the less moneyed, and the area underwent radical change. Excursion boats left Manhattan regularly for a day's outing. Great steel piers were built out into the water and the forerunner of the present boardwalk, which runs three miles and is 90 feet wide, was constructed. The amusement area grew into the extravaganza that made Coney Island famous throughout the world. Great amusement parks were built, such as Dreamland and Luna Park, seen by Maxim Gorky during his visit of 1906 and later described by him as "fabulous beyond conceiving." Steeplechase Park, built in 1897, survived until 1964, when its site was used for housing. The 250-foot parachute jump, the large umbrella-shaped tower left of center in the photo, was originally installed at the 1939 World's Fair in Flushing Meadows, Queens. Famous not only as a heart-stopping ride, it was the first recognizable structure in America sighted by soldiers from the decks of transport ships as they returned from Europe after World War II. Although steadily shrinking, the Coney Island midway still exists. The Cyclone roller coaster (center), which celebrated its fiftieth anniversary in 1977, is still a popular and exciting ride. The community at Coney Island is going through the throes of redevelopment. Large sections of older one- and two-family houses have been leveled to make way for public housing.

98. New York Aquarium, West 8th Street and Boardwalk, Coney Island. Octopuses slither, tiger sharks prowl and dolphins cavort in public view at the New York Aquarium. The public has delighted in the collection of 3,000 live aquatic specimens ever since the new facility, designed by Harrison & Abramovitz, opened in 1955. (Until the early 1940s the aquarium had been housed in Manhattan's Castle Clinton; see No. 2. Some of the fish were kept in the New York Zoological Park in the intervening years.) To most of the 500,000 landlubbers who visit each year, all the exhibits are wonderfully exotic, but some deserve special mention. There is a demonstration in which lightbulbs are illuminated with the power generated by electric eels. In the summer, dolphins perform routines to appreciative crowds. Children have the thrill of being able to touch ducks and handle smaller marine creatures such as horseshoe crabs. The collection, which is not entirely marine, includes freshwater specimens from North American lakes, streams, rivers and ponds. One of the most treasured displays is the Beebe bathysphere, used in making record-breaking depth dives in the 1930s.

99. Verrazano-Narrows Bridge. Reaching over the Narrows to join Staten Island with Brooklyn, the Verrazano-Narrows Bridge is the longest suspension bridge in the country. Its central span is 4,260 feet; the side spans are 1,215 feet each. The towers rise 690 feet above mean sea level. The sleek, graceful structure is the work of O. H. Ammann, designer of many bridges in the city, notably the George Washington, Throgs Neck and Triborough. Construction was started in 1959 and the bridge was opened to traffic on November 21, 1964. By 1972 the traffic load had reached 38,229,108 vehicles.

(Because usage was so much heavier than had been anticipated, a second deck was opened in 1969.) The bridge is named for Giovanni da Verrazano, an Italian explorer in the service of King Francois I of France. Verrazano sailed into New York Bay in 1524, preceding Henry Hudson by 85 years. The bridge has had considerable impact on Staten Island. It has encouraged industry to move to the island, has accelerated the growth of population there and thus has indirectly contributed to the gradual loss of the island's rustic quality.

100. Staten Island. Although it is more than twice the size of Manhattan (but with a population of only 330,000 in 1972), Staten Island is one of the least-known boroughs — a mystery to many New Yorkers. Perhaps this is because of its relative isolation: five miles across the harbor from Manhattan, it can be reached from New York only by the Staten Island Ferry from the Battery (see Nos. 1 and 5) or by the Verrazano-Narrows Bridge from Brooklyn. The first European to sight the island was Verrazano, who took on fresh water there in 1524. Early in the seventeenth century, when the Dutch occupied the area, it was named Staten Eylandt in honor of the Estates General, the legislative body of the Netherlands. When the English took it over in 1664, it was renamed Richmond after the Duke of Richmond, an illegitimate son of Charles II. Thus today, while it is normally called Staten Island, it is also the Borough of Richmond of the City of New York. At the outset of the Revolution, the island was politically Tory, as was New York City. In 1776 Lord Howe met with John Adams, Edward Rutledge and Benjamin Franklin at the Conference House (still standing) in Tottenville, at the southern end of the island, to discuss the possibility of a settlement of the "unpleasantness." His efforts came to nothing. Appropriately enough, the last shots of the Revolution were fired by nervous and irate British troops while evacuating Staten Island in 1783. A peaceful farming and fishing community, the island became popular with wealthy New Yorkers in the middle of the nineteenth century. James Russell Lowell spent time there, and Judge William Emerson had a house where he entertained his brother Ralph Waldo Emerson and Henry David Thoreau. Frederick Law Olmsted had a wheat farm on the island. Another New Yorker who moved there was John Austen. His granddaughter Alice grew up in his home Clear Comfort, which commands a splendid view of the Narrows. From 1880 until 1930 Alice Austen recorded much of Staten Island and New York in photographs that are a priceless legacy. She died in a nursing home in 1952, having been evicted from Clear Comfort. The house and land have since been acquired by the city, and a museum honoring her is being created there. The island is also noted as the place of refuge of Giuseppe Garibaldi between 1851 and 1853. The house in which he lived with his friend Antonio Meucci is preserved as a memorial to the great Italian unifier at Tompkins and Chestnut Avenues. The island contains a good deal of interesting architecture, ranging from Dutch farmhouses to the only Frank Lloyd Wright house in the city (on Lighthouse Avenue). Perhaps the most interesting architecture is to be found at the former Sailor's Snug Harbor on Richmond Terrace. The site for the complex, which served "aged, decrepit and worn-out sailors," was purchased in 1831 with funds left by Robert Richard Randall. The splendid Greek Revival main building, possibly the work of Minard Lafever, was built the same year. The flanking buildings were built later by Samuel Thompson and Son. Snug Harbor as an institution has since moved to North Carolina, but the city has purchased the old buildings and some of the land, preserving this unique complex. The view of Staten Island in the photograph shows St. George as seen from the approaching ferry.

101. John F. Kennedy International Airport, Queens. Kennedy Airport is one of the busiest in the world. Located 15 miles from Manhattan, the facility was opened in 1948 as Idlewild Airport and was renamed in 1963. Covering almost 5,000 acres of reclaimed Jamaica Bay marshland, Kennedy contains an air-cargo center, hangars and tower buildings devoted to maintenance and operations, administrative buildings, a hotel, garage and parking spaces, banks and other necessary services. The busiest section of the airport is the passenger-terminal area, covering 840 acres. Of the passenger-terminal buildings, the most successful architecturally is Eero Saarinen's Trans World Airlines Terminal, of which an interior area is shown here. Opened in 1962, it is a dazzling manipulation of form and space. The metropolitan area is also served by La Guardia Airport in Queens and Newark International Airport in New Jersey.

102. Belmont Park Race Track, Elmont, Nassau County.
Thrilled New Yorkers watch Seattle Slew, mounted by Jean Cruguet, thunder down the homestretch on his way to win the 1977 Belmont Stakes and capture the coveted Triple Crown. In the nineteenth century New Yorkers watched their thoroughbreds in competition at the tracks at Jerome Park and Morris Park in the Bronx, and at Brighton Beach in Brooklyn. In 1903 racing moved to Belmont Park, named after August Belmont, one of the leading members of New York society's horsey set and a founder of the Jockey Club, which still acts as a regulatory body of thoroughbred racing.

The track has since been completely renovated, and the grandstand now seats 30,000. Of the many prestigious races run on the mile-and-a-half track, the most famous remains the Belmont Stakes. The racing season in New York is now year-round, the time being divided among three tracks: Belmont, Aqueduct (in Ozone Park, Queens) and upstate at Saratoga during August. Horse fans can also attend the trotters at Roosevelt and Yonkers Raceways. Millions of dollars are bet at the tracks annually; millions more are waged at the Off-Track Betting parlors throughout New York. (*Photo courtesy NYRA Photos*)

INDEX

(References are to item numbers, not page numbers.)